homegrown PURE AND SIMPLE

homegrown PURE AND SIMPLE

great healthy food from garden to table

BY **MICHEL NISCHAN**

WITH MARY GOODBODY

PHOTOGRAPHS BY SUSIE CUSHNER

CHRONICLE BOOKS
SAN FRANCISCO

DEDICATION

Your whisper lies in the gentle rub of pea vines
against the trellis.

Your tender admonishments allow the beetles
to play where sufficient care was not taken.

The joy of your way fills my heart when
I see the wonder on the face of my children as they pull
giant carrots from the moist fall soil.

And your well-deserved rest is as pure and
promising as a fresh blanket of snow
over the beds that fed my family
and created a season of such wonderment.
The garden is the place we meet
and I'm glad we're still together.

For you, I have only one question:
why didn't you tell me about
those damned squash borers?
No worries, I'll let you know
when I figure it out for myself.

Thanks, Mom.

I couldn't have done it without you.

Text copyright © 2005 by Michel Nischan.
Photographs copyright © 2005 by Susie Cushner.
All rights reserved. No part of this book
may be reproduced in any form without
written permission from the publisher.

Library of Congress Cataloging-in-Publication
Data available.

ISBN 0-8118-4472-2

Manufactured in China

DESIGNED BY JULIA FLAGG
PROP STYLING BY HELEN CROWTHER
FOOD STYLING BY JEE LEVIN
PHOTOGRAPHER ACKNOWLEDGMENTS
The chemistry of our team, the location, the author and his exuberant
family created the synergy that inspired effortless flow. This project
came together with little time to spare. The vital elements rose to the
challenge with mastery, commitment, and a sense of humor like no other.
My sincere gratitude to VIVIEN SUNG, for providing the opportunity to
experience a project so unique; THE MATYIA FAMILY for opening their arms
and the warmth of their home as the space to create in; JEE LEVIN,
food stylist and tireless nurturer extraordinaire; HELEN CROWTHER's
discerning style, flair, and spontaneity, as well as her uncanny capacity to
keep us all in a constant state of laughter. To my sweet MAWGRIT, who
brought us to her home and assisted and organized my effort; and lovely
ALETA, for being a present, willing, and good-natured all-around help.
Finally, to MICHEL for his passion concerning growing and nurturing the
human spirit with healthful food, as well as his generosity throughout
the duration of our project. Thank you my dear friends.

Distributed in Canada by Raincoast Books
9050 Shaughnessy Street
Vancouver, British Columbia V6P 6E5

10 9 8 7 6 5 4 3 2 1

Chronicle Books LLC
85 Second Street
San Francisco, California 94105

www.chroniclebooks.com

CONTENTS

1   2   3   4

extending the
harvest

**side
dishes**

breakfast
and **breads**

desserts

5   6   7   8

INTRODUCTION

HOMAGE TO MY MOM
Feeling the love and a little bit of good ol' country

IF SOMEONE HAD TOLD ME TEN YEARS AGO THAT ONE DAY I WOULD RETURN TO THE COUNTRY COOKING OF MY CHILDHOOD, I wouldn't have believed them. At the time, I had refocused my cooking on health and well-being and was extremely excited about my new direction. I thought I would never look back, but that is exactly what has happened. I am absorbed by memories of my mother's country cooking.

Like my mom, I have a large vegetable garden, and like my mom, I cook simple, healthful meals for my family. The difference is that she knew only Southern country cooking—the cooking of her childhood. As a professional chef with white-tablecloth training, I have learned a lot about various cultures and sophisticated cooking methods. I cooked my way around the world without ever leaving my kitchen. Yet something inside me kept pulling at me to return "home." I have spent a decade silently struggling to reconcile my culinary heritage, which is down-home American country, with my desire to cook healthfully and to take good advantage of my excellent training. With this book, I have come to terms with all three elements.

You won't find recipes for fried chicken, ham and eggs, buttermilk biscuits, or coconut cake in these pages, but you will find homey dishes like TWO-SKILLET HERB-ROASTED CHICKEN WITH YUKON GOLD HOME FRIES (page 101) and ANGEL FOOD CAKE (page 209). In the spirit of my first book, *Taste: Pure and Simple,* you will find an abundance of wholesome dishes for chicken, pork, beef, and fish. I pair these with farm-fresh vegetables and vibrant herbs and spices, so that the ingredients practically shout with pure, full-bodied flavor.

This book is all about my mother and the way she cooked. It's also about how she influenced me so that I found my path and became a chef. The life I have now is one I couldn't imagine when I was growing up in Des Plaines, Illinois. Then my universe was my family, my school, and my friends. Now my universe embraces all the wonders of the world. I am blessed with a loving wife and five children, I have traveled the country and much of the globe, I have worked in some of the best restaurant kitchens in New York City and elsewhere, and I count some of the finest people in the food business among my dearest friends. Through it all, I always come back to Mom.

MY MOTHER, MYSELF

My mother was robbed of her birthright to be a farmer. She was born into a farm family in Missouri with generations of farmers preceding her. Working the land was in her blood, but life and the industrialization of agriculture took her to suburban Illinois, where she and my father raised my brothers, my sister, and me in a small house with a backyard planted with

vegetables right up to the sliding glass doors. It had not taken my mother long to decide that supermarkets were not for her when it came to fresh food for her family. She grew as many vegetables as she could in the backyard and fed us as she had been fed. What she couldn't grow, she bought at farm stands as far away from Des Plaines as Antioch, Illinois. In late spring, summer, and fall, we harvested fresh vegetables; in early spring and winter, we ate the canned, preserved, and frozen vegetables and fruits Mom had put up in the fall.

This is what I dream of doing for my growing family, too. With my new garden and with the commitment my wife, Lori, and I have to make it work for our kids and our lives, I know I will succeed.

While some chefs I know openly admit their mothers were not good cooks, many others insist they were magicians in the kitchen. I believe I have a leg up on the others because Mom *was* a farmer and a great cook, and anyone who doubts me is spouting blasphemy! All I have to do is prepare her recipes to convince even the most jaded critic. But is it healthful?

When I worked with the Association of Diabetes Educators on a recipe guide for Americans struggling with the daily challenges of diabetes, I submitted a recipe for smothered pork chops, cooked pretty much as my mother had cooked them. It came back from recipe testing with high marks, having met the dietary requirements for inclusion in the booklet. Why? Because the meat was served with plenty of fresh vegetables and the pork chops and serving amounts were smaller than in most contemporary recipes.

SUPPER-TABLE ECONOMICS

When Mom cooked smothered pork chops for us, the house filled up with tantalizing aromas that even wafted outside. We were *starving* by the time supper was on the table. Dad was the food cop. His rule was one pork chop per person until we tried a little of everything else: whole roasted cauliflower, collard greens, beans, home-canned tomatoes, and rice. We begged for a second chop. Heck, we thought we could eat a dozen chops! But in the end, those mighty tasty vegetables appeased our appetites.

Dad knew he was right. This was how he and Mom were raised growing up during the Depression. Meat was a luxury and never to be squandered. When we were young, money was tight for the family, and Dad's policing of the supper table was a matter of economics, which also kept us healthy and fit.

In those days, most people exercised similar common sense when it came to feeding families. For one thing, more families still farmed or were close to farming roots. Convenience foods may have been making inroads, but the way Americans actually cooked in the 1950s and 1960s was pretty close to how they had cooked in earlier decades. Freezers were not as efficient, kitchens had no microwaves, and supermarkets didn't offer the staggering array of packaged, prepared foods they do now. *Takeout* was not a noun and a delivered pizza was still a novelty.

In two short generations, we find ourselves removed from farming and the concept that goes along with it, which is one of frugality amid abundance. It is a way of life that not only makes good sense but also promotes good health. My friend Terrol Dew Johnson from the Tohono O'odham Nation, in Arizona and New Mexico, tells me that the wisdom of his ancestors is contained in a single tepary bean. It signifies how a society learned through trial and error which agricultural practices worked and which did not. Mistakes literally cost lives and could not afford to be repeated.

Our society has lost this connection to our food. I am dedicated to helping Americans find it again, and with the discovery, to respect our food and the people who produce it—particularly those who produce it sensibly and believe in good stewardship of the land. I truly believe we can fix our relationship with our food supply, even given that its complicated production and delivery system has gone bonkers.

For those who make the effort, food will taste better. When you start to eat meals that don't come from a drive-through window or a box heated in the microwave, your well-being becomes more secure—through fond food memories.

THE MISSING INGREDIENT

As I see my children grow up and as my own understanding of our agricultural heritage evolves, I yearn to return to the heirloom recipes I learned from my mother. When I wonder about their healthfulness and marvel at the comfort I find in their flavors, I remember one ingredient found in every single one: love.

When Mom taught me how to cook, she was passing on generations of love. This may sound corny, but the deposit of love in every dish is as rich as the deposits of minerals and nutrients in the good earth that nurtures our food. Every family member who passes on a recipe embellishes it with love. This may take the form of a respectful tweak in the method or streamlining the ingredients, but the love is there. Mom used to say, "Don't cook when you're unhappy. Someone will taste it and think you don't love them."

My heart has been aching to share simpler, down-to-earth recipes with my readers, recipes that rely on the bounty of gardens and local farms. My mission has long been to cook healthfully and so my conscience has, until now, held me in check from exploring these dishes. But now I see how I can do both.

As my mother would say, as long as your head is screwed on tight, you won't lose it. If you don't lose your head, you can do anything. I hope you're hungry!

CHAPTER

1

My garden
and how it
GREW

CHAPTER I

My Garden and How It Grew

LORI AND I STARTED OUR GARDEN IN AUGUST 2003, NEARLY A YEAR BEFORE THE FIRST SEED WAS PLANTED IN ITS SOIL. Our first season of cultivation began in spring 2004 and ended that fall, and, if I do say so, for a beginning garden, it was incredible. The next year promised to be even better. You can't rush a garden, but you can get enormous gratification from day one.

In reality, Lori and I started the garden years earlier. When we finally were ready to buy our first house, we knew what we wanted: The house had to be spacious enough to shelter our five kids, but sufficient land for a garden was equally important.

A FAMILY GARDEN

Our goal was to have an organic garden and to use all the vegetables we grow to feed our family. This is not as easy as it sounds. Anyone who has tended just a few zucchini or bean plants knows that springtime's exuberance can yield more food than you can eat. With careful planning and creative ways to extend the harvest—canning, freezing, drying, preserving (see chapter 6)—we will meet this goal someday. Until then, our garden teaches our kids other valuable lessons. Our two teenage daughters, Lauren and Courtney, have discovered joy in sharing our bounty with their friends' families. They are learning how food can be a gift and are developing a new sense of community that makes their friendships even deeper. Pretty amazing stuff!

Our teenage son, Chris, is a tremendous garden assistant, although he is not always first in line to help with heavy lifting. Truthfully, he would rather be grounded than grab the pitchfork and turn the compost pile, but once he joins me and we start working together, he appreciates the simple camaraderie and our joint sense of accomplishment.

I have explained to him that the future of the garden lies in the compost. As you add clippings, leaves, and other garden waste to the pile, it decomposes, valuable nutrients develop, and worms find a happy home. We compost all vegetable and fruit kitchen waste; nothing that contains meat, its by-products, sugar, or fat goes in the compost. Decomposed compost resembles dirt and is easy to work back into the soil, which it enriches so that the next year's crops are better than ever. Nothing speaks to the natural cycle of life better than a well-managed compost pile!

Chris is attuned to the value of the garden for a number of reasons. Being a growing, active teenager, he likes the food I cook from it, and he even admits to

enjoying working side by side with dear old dad, but I know above all he treasures the spirit of the project. When he was five years old, Chris was diagnosed with type 1 diabetes, a reality that forever changed the way I thought about and cooked food. Our youngest, Ethan, is diabetic, too, and so the good, healthful food we grow on our own property resonates with our entire family. We all value the benefits of responsibly raised, carefully tended food. Our lives depend on it.

Our two youngest boys, Andrew and Ethan, are as intrigued by the garden as I was by my mother's sprawling backyard plot. They spend hours with me, begging to pick vegetables before they are ripe, asking questions, and pulling stray weeds. If I let Ethan yank a few ripe carrots, he's thrilled, but as soon as I turn my back, he pulls another that might not be ready. I remember doing the same thing—and catching it from my mom when I did! I can't scold Ethan, though, and comfort myself with the knowledge that I am rinsing off carrots for him to eat, rather than opening a box of cookies.

YEARS OF PREPARATION

During the early '90s, as our family grew, we rented a number of houses along the way before we bought one, and we always made our landlords happy because inevitably we improved the property. Although we may not have owned the land, we enjoyed the process of cultivating it. When we look back at photographs of our kids from those years, it's gratifying to see them smiling in colorful flower gardens that we both recall tending, rather than standing on an anonymous plot of grass bordered by a chain-link fence.

During those early years, we used all the money we were able to save to start our own restaurant, a place called Miche Mache, first located in Norwalk and then in Stamford, Connecticut. After several fascinating and constructive years, the venture soured due to a disastrous partnership, and I began the next stage of my professional life: commuting by train from suburban Connecticut to Manhattan to work for the Myriad Restaurant Group, owned by Drew Nieporent and Michael Bonadies. The company is responsible for some of the best restaurants in the world: Montrachet, Layla, Heartbeat, and Tribeca Grill in New York; Nobu in New York and London; and Rubicon in San Francisco. Working with Drew and Michael was astonishing and I treasured every minute of it. After I had been with them for a year or so in various capacities, the two partners proposed opening a restaurant in a Manhattan hotel to match the "urban oasis" concept for the rest of the hotel, which included a spa, gyms, and serene guest rooms. The hotel was the W New York, and Drew suggested calling the restaurant Heartbeat, because it was destined to feature food for well-being. He also suggested I take it on. I agreed.

I was executive chef of Heartbeat from 1998 to 2002, and loved just about everything about the job. Drew is a culinary visionary whose energy and dedication are inspirational, and together we made tasty music! While at Heartbeat, I honed many of the techniques I use in my recipes today, significantly making the most of freshly juiced vegetables and fruits as integral ingredients and deepening my understanding of sustainable agriculture.

TIME FOR A HOUSE AND A GARDEN

In 2001, Lori and I agreed that the time was right—finally!—to buy a house.

From the street, our house doesn't look like much. It's a fairly ordinary brick ranch with a grassy front yard, but when you walk around to the back, a completely different story emerges. This is what sold us. We have a deep, gently sloping backyard that is, as it turns out, perfect for a large garden with room to spare for a growing, active family. We have a little more than an acre, which may be a premium in our coastal Connecticut town but which, in the scheme of things, is not a lot of land.

While our garden is large by conventional standards, you don't need as much land for a rewarding garden. But to reap those rewards, you need to plan your garden with care. Every farmer and gardener knows that soil, sun, and rain conspire so that crops grow. The farmer and gardener can control this collaboration with good planning, although in the end nature is the ultimate referee.

When you plan a garden, choose a site with enough sun and good drainage. Lori and I spent the first two years in our new house watching the patterns of the sun over the area we hoped to cultivate. We identified trees that needed felling and mapped out on paper and in our conversations how the garden would look. It's a luxury to spend time with a piece of property before you dig a garden, but a luxury worth indulging. Some places speak louder than others to the gardener, and you may find your first impressions are right on—or not. Frankly, half of the fun of a garden is watching it grow and mature over the years. It is an activity of hope and a sustaining of belief in the cycle of life.

THE GARDEN TAKES SHAPE

We were lucky. We had a good spot for the garden and knew our soil was organic because of the history of the place. Our next door neighbor, Florence Nichols Fensky, grew up on the land when it was still the Nichols farm. In 1947, the family subdivided the last ten acres of the property into eight building lots, and each one went to a family member. Everyone eventually built a house on the front end of the rectangular lots, near the street, leaving the far reaches of the lots to revert to woodland.

The tangle of scrub trees, brambles, and weeds that had taken over the back third of the yard was our chosen garden site. Whenever I could in 2002 and 2003, I was back there armed with a scythe, ax, shovel, and chainsaw, clearing the land, chopping down dead ash trees, and hacking away at those weeds known as poplar trees! I cut and stacked logs as they accumulated, with plans to use them in the garden. We piled the rest of the vegetation along the side of the yard where our compost pile now is. I dug out stones and rocks, many of which I used to build a stone wall for Lori's flower garden near the house, while others I earmarked for future use in the vegetable garden. We also found old household items like abandoned sinks and a refrigerator, and we unearthed cans, bottles, and other non-biodegradable things. These we hauled to the dump across town.

When we inspected our lawn, we knew it had grown in farmland soil. The grass was mixed with clover, smartweed, and rye, rather than being a lush, green thatch of fertilized suburban lawn. We were thrilled because this meant there had been no chemical inputs, which can seriously degrade the soil and the water table (we have one of the last remaining wells in our town, so we were doubly pleased).

Once the land was clear, we started outlining the future garden with string and chalk. Our major expense was to hire Peter Hoog, a friend who owns a backhoe. For a thousand dollars, he graded the back slope and leveled the land, following its natural contours, so that the garden was in three ascending sections. We used the heavy equipment to push the largest rocks in place to form a retaining wall.

There was a gorgeous oak tree at the back of the garden that had grown to magnificent proportions despite the scrub trees around it. With heavy hearts, we decided it had to go. It blocked too much sun. We kept the stump as a reminder of the tree's glory, and in summer, Lori festoons it with containers of flowers. It has become a favorite focal point in the garden.

I dug out five primary beds in the center of the garden and divided them by gravel paths. I dug down and then built up the beds, surrounding each one with walls made from ash logs. Because we live in a region of the country with a lot of rainfall, we decided on raised beds. Connecticut can easily get more than forty-five inches of rain a year, and while we are not strangers to summer droughts, we get full days of unrelenting, pelting rain, particularly in the spring.

I didn't want my seedlings to wash away or their roots to rot! Raised beds provide protection, good drainage, and, when you dig down a foot or so into the earth below them, ample room for root development.

I used the ash logs to contain the raised beds for a few reasons. First, they were there, which saved us money. Second, they were organic and because I am working toward a fully organic garden, I had no interest in treated lumber. Third, while they will rot eventually, they are thick enough to last for a number of years before termites and exposure get the best of them. By then, I hope to have the time and energy to surround my mature raised beds with rocks. And finally, they look cool! I used logs from the felled trees to make benches for the garden, too.

I dug French drains along the sides of the beds. These are shallow trenches filled with gravel and loose soil that channel excess water away from the beds. I then got to work on the soil.

THE GARDEN'S SOIL

I took a sample of the soil to the Connecticut Agricultural Experiment Station. Agricultural departments in most states run similar centers where, for a modest fee, you can have your soil tested. Our test indicated we were in very good shape, although a little heavy in the clay department and missing some nutrients.

I ordered a load of certified organic loam and mulch from a company called Sweet Peet in nearby New York State (see page 221 for more information). The folks there produce a 100 percent organic product from soil, manure, and other ingredients they get from local farms. After some research, I decided it would be a good soil builder. Late in summer 2003, I spread the loam over the dug, raised beds, mixed it with organic mulch and loam, covered the beds with straw, and left the soil alone until the following spring. During those months, the soil decomposed and attracted worms. Nutrients grew and the soil was in good shape for planting by spring.

I had the soil tested again. The experiment station suggested I add chicken compost, bonemeal, and cottonseed meal. I amended the soil with the first two suggestions and disregarded the last, mainly because organic cottonseed meal is hard to find and expensive. I bought my own soil-testing kit and, after some more amending, the ground was ready for planting.

Nearly everything in the garden was and is started from organic seed, most of it bought from Seeds of Change, a New Mexico–based company dedicated to preserving heirloom vegetables and fruits, to safeguarding biodiversity, and to promoting sustainable, organic agriculture (see page 221 for more information). A number of seed companies sell organic seeds and plants and focus on heirloom vegetables, and they are worth seeking out. I did rely on seedlings for tomatoes, eggplant, and Swiss chard. I plan one day to build a small greenhouse in which I can germinate plants from seeds I harvest from my own vegetables.

MY MOTHER AND MY GARDEN

I never deny my mother's influence when I work in the garden. I hear her voice in my ear when, like Ethan, I reach for a vegetable that is not quite ripe just because . . . I sense her presence when I am tempted to cut corners or quit before the chores are done. I value the lessons she taught me about patience, hard work, and reaping a bountiful harvest. Her wisdom nourishes my soul as I labor for long hours over my beds, back aching, neck tight from sunburn, and still never enough hours in the day. As I walk back to the house, ready for a cool drink and hot shower, I smile happily as memories of her skitter through my mind. In some ways, I feel closer to her now more than ever.

After my mom died in September 2002, I went back to work at Heartbeat, following a short period of mourning. The urge to quit my job overwhelmed me in those weeks, and I sensed that the restaurant kitchen was not where I belonged. I found it wearing to convince the hotel managers—yet again—that buying food directly from farmers in an effort to support sustainable agriculture was the way to go. The battles were familiar ones, and I felt I had lost this particular war. My oldest daughter, Lauren, was in her last year of high school and soon would be off to college; my youngest son was leaving his babyhood behind. It was time to start a new chapter that involved my kids and satisfied my intense longing to build a garden.

I credit my mother with giving me the strength to embark on this crazy pursuit, and my wife with lending her unqualified support. Lori and I decided I could rely on writing, speaking, and consulting to make ends meet, and so I hung up my chef's jacket and grabbed the hoe and shovel.

We're only beginning, but I know the endeavor will continue for years to come. Welcome to my garden!

CHAPTER
2

salads

WHEN LORI AND I DECIDED TO PLANT A LARGE VEGETABLE GARDEN, WE WERE NOT DOING IT TO FEED THE DEER. This meant building a ten-foot-high deer fence, and because I am not a fence builder, I turned to my friend Bruno Gallace for help. He suggested untreated hemlock logs for fence posts, and when it came time to raise the posts, our neighbors came over to help. The afternoon resembled an old-fashioned barn raising. Afterward I fired up my six-foot-long grill and cooked a "fence-raising" feast. I grilled spring vegetables alongside RIB-EYE STEAKS WITH SAVORY HERBS AND ROASTED GARLIC (page 83) and GRILLED LAMB CHOPS WITH HOME-DRIED TOMATOES AND CITRUS YOGURT (page 85), and in the cool spring evening, everything tasted fantastic.

Our next task was to plant the garden so that it would be as lush and summery as possible by the end of May, when an international magazine was scheduled to photograph it for an article on a summer garden in the September issue. I knew that the only vegetables that would be ready to photograph by late May would be lettuces, radishes, and peas, so I immediately cried for help. I turned to dear friend Peter Stephens of Elegant Effects in Fairfield, Connecticut. Peter is a renowned gardener whose work has been featured in many well-known publications. If anyone could help, he could. Peter immediately suggested planting a variety of lettuces throughout the garden, mixing them in with other spring plants so that the garden would achieve a fullness most early gardens don't have.

I also turned to Dave and Ainsley Jackson, the owners of Enterprise organic farm in South Deerfield, Massachusetts, who extend their growing seasons by planting in large greenhouses. They invited Lori and me to select some plants, and we drove home with an array of vegetables we hoped would help the garden appear more summerlike. We worked day and night (two nights under a full moon) to plant everything.

In the end, the photo shoot didn't work out exactly as planned. The magazine's art director sensibly focused on tight shots; the garden was just not lush enough to pass for summertime. The good news was we had fourteen varieties of wonderful heirloom lettuces and an astonishing array of radishes and peas. Needless to say, we ate a lot of salads that spring. An unexpected bonus was that the garden was so luxuriant and verdant by midsummer that many seasoned gardeners couldn't believe it was a first-year garden.

TANGY AUTUMN GREENS
with Honey-Roasted Walnuts, Dried Cherries, and Stilton Cheese

SERVES
4

SALADS SHOULD NEVER BE AFTERTHOUGHTS. They round out a meal with their vibrant flavors and deliver needed fiber to the daily diet. Rich, dark greens, such as arugula and mustard, are good choices for fiber and, because they are not quickly digested, help you feel satisfied longer. Having spent the summer in the sun, these autumn greens are nutritionally powerful and boldly flavored. I add blue-veined Stilton cheese for its rich creaminess (not to mention abundant calcium and protein!), dried cherries for their super tart acidity, and nuts for crunchiness. Cheese, nuts, fruit—what could be better?

½ **CUP FRESHLY PRESSED APPLE JUICE** or apple cider

½ **CUP BALSAMIC VINEGAR**

¼ **CUP DRIED CHERRIES**

I **TEASPOON EXTRA-VIRGIN OLIVE OIL**

6 CUPS ASSORTED FULL-FLAVORED SALAD GREENS such as arugula, frisée, dandelion, and mustard

I **SMALL RED ONION**, thinly sliced

¼ **CUP CHOPPED HONEY-ROASTED WALNUTS** (page 24)

¼ **TO** ⅓ **CUP CRUMBLED STILTON CHEESE**

SALT AND FRESHLY GROUND BLACK PEPPER

I. In a small saucepan or sauté pan, combine the apple juice and vinegar and bring to a simmer over medium heat. Put the cherries in a heatproof bowl and pour the hot liquid over them. Set aside to soften for 30 minutes.

2. Pour the cherries and their soaking liquid through a sieve held over the original pan and set the cherries aside. Bring the liquid to a simmer over medium heat and reduce to ¼ cup. It will be syrupy. Pour the syrup into a small bowl and whisk in the oil. Whisk again briefly before using.

3. In a large bowl, combine the greens, onion, walnuts, and softened cherries. Sprinkle with the cheese and season lightly with salt and pepper. Drizzle the slightly warm dressing over the salad. Toss gently so that the cheese does not break down or clump.

4. Divide the salad among 4 chilled plates and serve immediately.

honey-roasted walnuts

MAKES ABOUT I CUP

½ CUP LOCAL HONEY

¼ CUP RAW CANE SUGAR

½ TEASPOON COARSE
SEA SALT

⅛ TO ¼ TEASPOON CAYENNE
PEPPER

I CINNAMON STICK

I CUP UNBROKEN
WALNUT HALVES

I. Preheat the oven to 350°F.

2. In a small, heavy saucepan, combine the honey, sugar, salt, cayenne, and cinnamon stick over medium heat. Bring to a simmer, stir once, and let cook for a few minutes, or until the sugar dissolves.

3. Add the walnuts to the pan, stir to coat, and simmer for 5 to 7 minutes, or until lightly browned. Drain the walnuts through a sieve or colander. Discard the cinnamon stick.

4. Place a wire rack on a rimmed baking sheet or line the baking sheet with a nonstick baking liner. Spread the walnuts on the rack or liner. Roast for 8 to 10 minutes, or until the nuts darken slightly. The walnuts will not be crispy at this point.

5. Let the walnuts cool completely on the rack or liner. They will turn crisp as they cool. Use immediately or store in an airtight container for up to 6 days.

WHY LOCAL HONEY?

Whenever possible, I prefer honey to other sweeteners. You can't substitute it for granulated sugar in baking recipes, but when you need to sweeten a dressing, sauce, or similar preparation, a drizzle of honey works wonders. I always specify "local honey" for a few reasons.

First, buying honey from local producers, who very often have small operations, supports local agriculture, a concept I champion. Second, while you can't designate any honey as "organic" because no one can control where honeybees gather nectar, local producers know more about their honey than large commercial operations do. Third, studies indicate that eating local honey may increase your immunity to airborne allergens. It also means it might turn granular during storage, but this is harmless. Set the jar in a pan of hot water and the honey will liquefy.

The flavor and color of honey has nothing to do with its processing. These characteristics are dependent on the flowers available to the bees. In general, light-colored honey is more delicate tasting than dark honey. Clover, lavender, and orange-blossom honey are light; buckwheat, tupelo, and eucalyptus are darker. Local honey is apt to taste best with the fruits and vegetables that flourish in the same region.

The best places to shop for honey in your area are local farmers' markets and small groceries. It's easier to find than you might think—just look! It keeps for about a year, but I doubt storage will be a problem.

Osaka
MUSTARD GREENS
Salad

SERVES
6

I LOVE TO GROW THESE TENDER PURPLE-LEAVED MUSTARD GREENS IN MY GARDEN. They are particularly pretty and also do well planted right alongside flowers in window boxes and large containers. Their official name is Osaka, so when you order seeds, use it. You can find the greens in farmers' markets as well. The small leaves, packed with vitamins and antioxidants, have been used in Asian cultures for millennia, for both healing and eating. If you find them too pungent by themselves—they do have a pleasingly sharp flavor—mix them with milder greens or use them in your own mesclun mix. If you can't find them, use the smallest, most tender mustard greens in the market. They are lovely with roasted peppers and sweet onions.

2 TABLESPOONS CIDER VINEGAR

I TABLESPOON FRESH LIME JUICE

2 TABLESPOONS GRAPESEED OIL

SALT AND FRESHLY GROUND BLACK PEPPER

4 OUNCES OSAKA PURPLE MUSTARD LEAVES, other small red mustard leaves, or leaves from the center of a large bunch (about 6 cups loosely packed)

3 RED BELL PEPPERS, roasted, peeled, and seeded (see Note), then cut into ¼-inch-wide julienne

½ SMALL SWEET ONION such as Vidalia or Walla Walla, sliced paper-thin

¼ CUP ½-INCH-LONG FRESH CHIVES

I. In a salad bowl, whisk together the vinegar and lime juice. Whisk in the oil and season to taste with salt and pepper. You will have about ⅓ cup dressing.

2. Add the mustard leaves, bell peppers, onion, and chives to the bowl and toss to mix. Adjust the seasoning and serve immediately.

NOTE: You can roast whole peppers on a charcoal or gas grill, under the broiler, or over a gas flame. Set them over (or under) the heat and cook until the skins begin to char. Turn with tongs and continue grilling until charred on all sides. Watch the peppers closely, as they cook quickly. Using tongs to turn them prevents them from splitting open and losing moisture. When evenly charred, transfer them immediately to a container just large enough to hold them. Cover tightly with plastic wrap and let the peppers cool to the touch. Using your fingertips, rub the charred skin off the peppers. Split lengthwise, remove the seeds and ribs, and cut as directed in individual recipes.

WATERMELON, ARUGULA,
and Toasted Almond Salad

SERVES
6

YOU MIGHT GROW WATERMELON IN YOUR GARDEN but more likely you will buy it at a farm stand or market. I like to encourage even beginner gardeners to grow their own and think of it as ground cover. Instead of a couple flats of impatiens, plant watermelon seeds on a sunny side of the house and watch them take over. I recommend a type called Moon and Stars for its gorgeous green leaves marked with little yellow spots and its rich, juicy flesh. The dark green melons have brighter yellow spots, which explain the name.

If you don't grow your own, buy a small melon that feels heavy and full of juice and then, when you cut off the outer slices, you will notice that most of the seeds are in the center, or heart. Most people think of watermelon as a one-dimensional fruit, eating it plain as dessert or a sweet snack. But it's also good in a savory salad.

The Italians discovered how rich it tastes when very slightly heated; its flavors meld beautifully. Even raw watermelon tastes great with almonds, and we already know that arugula, radishes, and scallions complement one another. Put them all together and bank on the premise that opposite flavors attract. It works!

continued

watermelon, arugula, and toasted almond salad

continued

I SMALL WATERMELON
(about 6 pounds)

SALT

½ CUP EXTRA-VIRGIN OLIVE OIL

**¼ CUP BALSAMIC
OR CIDER VINEGAR**

FRESHLY GROUND BLACK PEPPER

3 OUNCES ARUGULA LEAVES
(about 4 cups loosely packed)

**⅔ CUP SLIVERED BLANCHED
ALMONDS**, lightly toasted

¼ CUP SLICED SCALLIONS,
white and green parts

12 RED RADISHES,
thinly sliced (about 1¼ cups)

I. To peel the watermelon, slice off both ends to reveal the flesh. Stand the watermelon upright on a cutting board. Using a large knife, slice the rind from the flesh, working from the top to the bottom in one long slice if possible. Repeat, using the white of the rind as a guide for the knife, until the melon is completely peeled. Cut the flesh into 2-inch-thick slices and set aside the rounded end cuts. Trim the slices into shapes that will fit on the serving platter you plan to use (I like diamonds). Reserve the heart (center) of the melon. Season each slice with salt and, using ¼ cup of the olive oil, brush one side of each slice.

2. Heat a large skillet or griddle over medium heat. When hot, working in batches, place the watermelon slices, oiled side down, on the hot skillet and leave for about 45 seconds, or until heated. With a large spatula or tongs, remove the slices, heated side up, to a chilled plate.

3. Put the reserved heart of the melon and the rounded end pieces in a sieve over a bowl and smash with your hands or a stiff whisk, forcing the juice into the bowl. Measure 1 cup of the juice (drink the rest or freeze it into ice cubes).

4. In a saucepan, combine the vinegar and watermelon juice. Bring to a boil over medium-high heat, reduce the heat to medium, and simmer, uncovered, for about 15 minutes, or until reduced to about ¼ cup.

5. Pour the reduced juice into a serving bowl and whisk in the remaining ¼ cup oil. Season to taste with salt and pepper. Add the arugula, almonds, scallions, and radishes and toss well. Gently mound the arugula salad over the melon slices and serve.

Simple
GREEN SALAD
with Lemon-Herb Vinaigrette

SERVES
6

EVERY RESTAURANT CHEF FACES THE CHALLENGE OF MAKING SIMPLE GREEN SALADS INTERESTING. Home cooks, too, find them a tad boring, but no one disputes that everyone enjoys them. If you grow a variety of greens in your garden, your salads will be far more appealing. Here, I use buttery Bibb lettuce, but you could use any soft greens. Splash them with Meyer lemon or other citrus juice to lend creativity without making the salad unapproachable. A little lemon oil (extra-virgin olive oil infused with lemon) is nice, too. If you can't find Meyer lemons, which are sweeter than ordinary lemons and are at their peak from November through May, use grapefruit.

**2 TABLESPOONS PLUS
I TEASPOON FRESH MEYER
LEMON JUICE** or pink grapefruit
juice

**2 TEASPOONS FRESH
LEMON JUICE**

**I TEASPOON EXTRA-VIRGIN
LEMON OLIVE OIL**

**I TEASPOON CHOPPED
FRESH FLAT-LEAF PARSLEY**

**I TEASPOON CHOPPED
FRESH CHERVIL**

**I TEASPOON CHOPPED
FRESH CHIVES**

**SALT AND FRESHLY GROUND
BLACK PEPPER**

**LEAVES FROM 3 HEADS
BIBB LETTUCE**

4 MEYER LEMONS, peeled and
segmented, or I pink grapefruit, peeled,
segmented, and each segment cut into
3 pieces (see Note)

I. In a small bowl, whisk the Meyer and regular lemon juice with the oil. Add all the herbs and season to taste with salt and pepper. Whisk again briefly before using.

2. To assemble, place 1 large lettuce leaf in the center of each of 6 chilled salad plates. Brush each leaf with some of the dressing and top with a few lemon segments. Select the next 6 largest leaves and lay them on top of the lemons. Brush with more dressing and top with more lemon segments. Repeat until you have used all the lettuce and fruit. You will have a stack of lettuce leaves on each plate. Drizzle with the remaining dressing and serve immediately.

NOTE: To segment the grapefruit, cut a slice off the top and bottom. Stand the fruit upright and cut downward to remove the pith and peel, following the contour of the fruit. Holding the fruit in your hand, cut along the membrane on both sides of each segment, freeing the segments and capturing them in a bowl.

Stack-of-Many-Vegetables
SALAD

**SERVES
4**

ON ONE OF MY TRIPS TO INDIA, I was asked to prepare two special dinners to showcase my pure and simple cuisine, one in Mumbai and one in New Delhi. The organizers requested that at least 45 percent of the food appeal to vegetarians. That would be unheard of in the United States, where a chef might plan on 5 percent of the menu being vegetarian-friendly. Had I known before I arrived that the percentage would be so large, I would have planned a three-course menu, but I had promised five courses. When I landed in Mumbai, I had to make some adjustments.

First, I nixed the salad course. My client told me that many Indians don't eat raw greens. To get some ideas for changing the menu, I took an early morning trip to Crawford Market, the large, bustling produce market in the middle of the city. As I wandered through the stalls, I grabbed foods that appealed to me. In particular, I was drawn to the baby corn, which you also see in Southeast Asia. Indian chefs often soak vegetables in buttermilk or yogurt and then dry them. I tried my own twist by marinating the corn in yogurt and then roasting the ears. I also gravitated toward the long chawli beans, which are common in India. (Some growers in Massachusetts cultivate them, but they are not easy to find, so Chinese long beans can be used in their place.)

For a dressing that would both satisfy my need that it be healthful and play to the sweet, powerful flavor preference of the Indian palate, I turned to small, beautiful plums. The final result was this architecturally stunning dish, where the beans, carrots, and corn can be stacked like Lincoln Logs and the very small amount of greens act primarily as a garnish. Not actually a salad, but close enough.

**½ CUP ORGANIC PLAIN
WHOLE-MILK YOGURT**

2 TEASPOONS MASALA SPICE

8 EARS BABY CORN,
shucked and split lengthwise (see Note)

I CUP CORN KERNELS
(from 2 to 3 medium ears)

FRESH LIME JUICE, if needed

6 RED PLUMS,
halved and pitted

3 GREEN CARDAMOM PODS

I SMALL CINNAMON STICK

**3 OR 4 SLICES FRESH CHILI
PEPPER,** green, red, or both

I TABLESPOON GRAPESEED OIL

**SALT AND FRESHLY GROUND
BLACK PEPPER**

4 YARD-LONG BEANS, chawli beans,
or any long green beans, stems trimmed,
blanched, shocked in ice water, and split
lengthwise (see Note)

**I LARGE OR 2 MEDIUM
RED CARROTS,** peeled and cut into
batons about the size of the split corn

I WHITE RADISH (DAIKON),
peeled and cut into batons about the
size of the split corn

**2 CUPS ASSORTED SMALL
LETTUCE LEAVES**

**SALT AND FRESHLY GROUND
BLACK PEPPER**

1. In a shallow nonreactive bowl, mix together the yogurt and masala spice. Add the baby corn and turn to coat. Cover and refrigerate for at least 1 hour or up to 2 hours.

2. Preheat the oven to 375°F.

3. Juice the corn kernels in a heavy-duty juicer. Remove the pulp from the juicer, wrap it in cheesecloth, and, holding it over the corn juice, squeeze the pulp to extract as much juice as possible. You will have about ⅓ cup juice.

4. In a small saucepan, heat the corn juice over medium heat, stirring gently and constantly, for 4 to 6 minutes, or until it thickens. Reduce the heat to low and cook until the starch cooks out and the sauce now thins a little. It should be the consistency of lightly beaten egg yolks. Depending on the season, the corn may need to be thinned with lime juice or water. Set aside to cool.

5. Juice the plums in the juicer. You will have about 3 cups juice. Set aside.

6. In a saucepan or skillet, toast the cardamom pods and cinnamon stick over medium heat for about 30 seconds, or until fragrant and lightly browned.

7. Reduce the heat, add the plum juice and chili slices (use more or fewer slices depending on their heat), and simmer for 25 to 30 minutes, or until reduced to about ¼ cup. The mixture will have a syrupy consistency. Strain through a fine-mesh sieve into a bowl and set aside to cool.

continued

stack-of-many-vegetables salad

continued

8. When the plum syrup is cool, whisk in the oil to make the dressing. Season to taste with salt and pepper and set aside until needed. Lift the baby corn from the marinade and discard the marinade. Lay the corn on a baking sheet and roast, turning several times, for about 12 minutes, or until lightly browned.

9. Arrange the roasted corn, beans, carrots, and radish in the center of each of 4 plates.

10. Put the lettuce leaves in a bowl and drizzle a teaspoon or two of the plum dressing over the lettuce. Toss well and tuck into the center of each vegetable stack. Drizzle the plate with the cooled corn sauce and the remaining plum dressing.

NOTES: Fresh baby corn is the same size as the little ears packed in a mild brine in cans and jars. It's available at farmers' markets from early to late summer, and if you can't find it, request it. You can use the canned variety, which won't be as tasty. If you do, be sure to drain and rinse it well before marinating it.

To blanch the beans, bring water to a depth of an inch or two to a boil over high heat. Add the beans and cook for 1 to 2 minutes, or until bright green and barely tender. Drain and immediately plunge in ice water to shock and stop the cooking. Drain again.

SUGAR SNAP PEAS
with Fennel, Onions, and Grilled Peach Dressing

SERVES
4

THIS SIMPLE DISH MAKES GOOD USE OF SOME OF SUMMER'S FINEST CROPS: sugar snap peas, sweet onions, and peaches. Where you might want to see clematis or climbing roses in a garden, try peas. The tendrils twist and wind up lattices and fences to make a great show, and soon after the pea flowers are spent, you can harvest the sweet, tender peas. Sugar snaps are meant to be eaten whole, without shelling. Trim their stems and string them only if necessary. I also love the vibrancy of raw, shelled sweet peas.

I will always remember the late spring of 2004 as the time that my three-year-old son Ethan fell in love with Sweet Marvel peas. I let him pick them and showed him how to open the pods and eat the sweet morsels inside. For a few weeks, he asked every morning if we could go pick peas. He was enthralled with the concept that food grew in the garden. Lori and I kept the

peas in the ground for as long as we could—well into the summer, past their prime—and on the day we finally pulled the plants to plant something else, Ethan sobbed and stomped his feet. In a stroke of motherly brilliance, Lori reminded him how much he liked carrots, and I steered him to the beds where the first small carrots were ready for pulling. He was happy again!

Peaches pair magnificently with peas. Their seasons sometimes meet, with peaches beginning as the peas are ending; in some places, they actually coincide. Use very juicy peaches for this dressing. Grilling intensifies their flavor and the salt extracts their juices, so that when they are mixed with the honey and piquant sherry vinegar, they conspire to create a dressing that happily pairs with both the peas and the sweet, aromatic fennel.

continued

sugar snap peas with fennel, onions, and grilled peach dressing

continued

3 RIPE BUT FIRM PEACHES, halved and pitted

SALT

2 TABLESPOONS EXTRA-VIRGIN OLIVE OIL

¼ CUP SHERRY VINEGAR

2 TEASPOONS LOCAL HONEY

FRESHLY GROUND BLACK PEPPER

4 CUPS SUGAR SNAP PEAS (about 14 ounces), trimmed

I FENNEL BULB (about 8 ounces)

I CUP SHELLED SWEET MARVEL PEAS or other sweet shell peas

½ CUP SHAVED SWEET ONION such as Vidalia or Walla Walla (see Note)

¼ CUP SLICED FRESH CHERVIL LEAVES

¼ CUP SLICED FRESH FLAT-LEAF PARSLEY LEAVES

¼ CUP I-INCH-LONG FRESH CHIVES

I. Prepare a charcoal or gas grill for grilling over a medium-hot fire. If using charcoal, mound the coals to one side of the grill in preparation for indirect grilling. If using a gas grill, turn one of the burners to low. Lightly oil the grill grate. Alternatively, you can use a countertop grill, such as a George Foreman grill.

2. Season the flesh side of each split peach with salt and rub lightly with a little of the oil. Place the peaches, flesh side down, on the grill rack over the hottest part of the fire and cook for 1 to 2 minutes, or until you can see nice grill marks. Using tongs, move the peach halves to the cooler part of the grill, turn them over so that the skin sides are facing down, and grill for about 3 minutes, or until warmed through. Remove the peaches from the grill and, when cool enough to handle, slide off the skins.

3. Using a paring knife, remove any small pieces of skin clinging to the peaches and then cut them into ½-inch cubes. Put the peaches in a glass or ceramic bowl and add the vinegar, honey, and remaining oil. Toss gently, season to taste with salt and pepper, toss again, and set aside to macerate for 1 hour.

4. When ready to serve, fill a saucepan with water, season to taste with salt and pepper, and bring to a boil. Add the sugar snap peas and blanch for 1 to 2 minutes. Drain the peas and immediately plunge them into ice water to shock and stop the cooking. Drain and add to the bowl with the peaches.

5. Shave the fennel bulb on the large holes of a handheld grater or with a knife. You will have about 2 cups. Add the fennel, shelled peas, onion, chervil, parsley, and chives to the peaches, toss well, season to taste with salt and pepper, and serve immediately.

NOTE: I usually shave onions on the large holes of a handheld grater or with a small knife.

CUCUMBER, BUSH BEAN, and TOMATO SALAD with Feta Cheese

**SERVES
6 TO 8**

MY FAMILY OF SEVEN CAN GO THROUGH A LOT OF BEANS IN A SHORT TIME, and so when I planted the garden, I made sure that the harvest would be ample. There's really no difference between bush and pole beans once they are picked and cooked; the distinction comes in how they grow. Bush beans are easy to get at, since they grow on low-lying bushes, but the bushes take up space. Pole beans grow up trellises, fences, or, not surprisingly, poles. Once they reach the top, they will tumble down over themselves. Keep this in mind when you buy or build support trellises. If they are too high, you might find yourself on a ladder anchored in soft garden dirt, trying to reach for the beans—not a good idea! You can sow other climbing plants alongside the pole beans to turn the trellis or fence into a prettier place. Lori planted climbing black-eyed Susans and morning glories with my pole beans so that lively yellow, orange, and blue flowers could poke their heads out from the vines and say a warm "hello!"

SALT

8 OUNCES ASSORTED POLE
OR BUSH BEANS such as green,
purple, and yellow wax beans, stems
trimmed and any strings removed

3 CUCUMBERS
such as Kirby or lemon

I SMALL RED ONION,
thinly sliced

8 OUNCES FETA CHEESE

3 LARGE VINE-RIPENED
TOMATOES

2 TO 3 TABLESPOONS
FRESH OREGANO LEAVES

½ CUP LOOSELY PACKED,
THINLY SLICED FRESH BASIL
LEAVES

¼ CUP EXTRA-VIRGIN OLIVE OIL

FRESHLY GROUND BLACK PEPPER

3 TABLESPOONS MALT VINEGAR

1. Fill a large saucepan with water, add salt, and bring to a boil. Taste the water before it heats up to make sure it's in balance and does not taste too salty. First add any green and/or wax beans you are using and blanch for 1 minute. Next, add purple beans (if using) and cook for 30 seconds longer. Drain the beans and immediately plunge them into ice water to shock and stop the cooking. Drain and pat the beans between clean kitchen towels or paper towels to remove excess water. Cut the beans in half crosswise. Refrigerate until chilled.

2. Peel the cucumbers, if desired, cut in half lengthwise, and seed. Then cut into 1½-inch cubes. Chill the cucumbers and the onion slices.

3. Meanwhile, use a fork to break the feta into chucks about half the size of the cubed cucumbers.

4. Core the tomatoes and cut into 1½-inch chunks. In a large bowl, mix the tomatoes with the feta cheese. Add the oregano, basil, and chilled beans, cucumber, and onion slices.

5. Drizzle with the oil and season to taste with salt and pepper. Add the vinegar and toss gently. Adjust the seasoning and serve.

CHAPTER
3

soups

WITHOUT QUESTION, SOUPS ARE YEAR-ROUND PLAYERS THAT CAN HIGHLIGHT THE WONDERS OF THE GARDEN IN EVERY SEASON. Many people think of soups mainly in the fall and winter, but, to me, soup is always the best representation of where we are in the calendar. Think of tomato soup in the summer, pea soup in the spring, or squash soup in the fall. You have to work a lot harder to bring a season to the table when you're roasting a rock cod or a chicken than when you are making soup. Indeed, when one of these proteins is featured as the centerpiece of the meal, the season is generally revealed in the vegetable accompaniment—or in the soup that precedes the main course.

For a rich, full-bodied fall soup or a lighter, more refreshing summer soup, you never have to manipulate the main ingredient very much to yield a satisfying result. In fact, the best soups inevitably focus on a single seasonal ingredient that reflects the bounty of the garden on the day the soup is served.

PUMPKIN SOUP
with Crispy Sage Garnish

**SERVES
6**

WHEN I TALK ABOUT PUMPKIN, I AM REFERRING TO WHAT A LOT OF FOLKS CALL WINTER SQUASHES: Hubbard, kabocha, and butternut, to name a few of the most popular, as well as the orange squash we call a pumpkin and associate most readily with Halloween. You may grow any of these squashes in the garden, or you may prefer to buy them at a roadside stand, but either way, don't pass them by. Small orange pumpkins are terrific for a lot more than Thanksgiving pies.

I love this smooth, creamy pumpkin soup made without a drop of cream. I add cinnamon, which loves pumpkin, but then play off the resulting autumnal flavors by bringing in savories such as chili peppers and cardamom. Cinnamon, chilies, and cardamom are used throughout South Asia and Southeast Asia, as are a number of pumpkins. Foods that originate in the same region of the world generally taste good together, and while neither squashes nor chilies are native to Asia, they have long been integral to its multiple cuisines. Interestingly, chilies were introduced to Asia by the Portuguese, who brought them from the New World. It didn't take long for the Asians or the Portuguese to figure out what to do with them.

I love the cardamom because it's unexpected—a "What did you put in this?" kind of flavor that makes this soup especially fun to serve. Frying sage does two wonderful things: it multiplies the flavor of the sage already in the soup, and it adds great, crispy texture. The leaves smell and taste great, too.

continued

pumpkin soup
with crispy sage garnish

continued

ONE 3-POUND PUMPKIN
or Hubbarb squash, peeled, seeded,
and cut into 1-inch cubes

2 TABLESPOONS OLIVE OIL

**SALT AND FRESHLY GROUND
BLACK PEPPER**

1 SWEET ONION such as Vidalia
or Walla Walla, cut into ½-inch-thick slices

6 CLOVES GARLIC,
split lengthwise

**¼ CUP PLUS 2 TEASPOONS
GRAPESEED OIL**

3 GREEN CARDAMOM PODS
or ½ teaspoon ground cardamom

2 CINNAMON STICKS

**½ SMALL RED THAI
OR JALAPEÑO CHILI,**
seeded and thinly sliced

**4 CUPS HOMEMADE OR CANNED
VEGETABLE OR CHICKEN STOCK**

**1 TABLESPOON THINLY SLICED
FRESH SAGE LEAVES,** plus 12 large
whole leaves

1. Preheat the oven to 350°F.

2. In a large bowl, toss the pumpkin cubes with the olive oil and a generous amount of salt and pepper. Spread the pumpkin evenly on a rimmed baking sheet and roast for about 25 minutes, or until nearly tender when pricked with a fork.

3. Meanwhile, coat the onion slices and the garlic with the 2 teaspoons grapeseed oil. When the pumpkin is ready, make room on the baking sheet for the onion and garlic, and return the pan to the oven for about 15 minutes longer, or until the pumpkin and onion are tender. Keep an eye on the garlic and turn, if necessary, to keep it from turning dark. Transfer all the vegetables to a large saucepan.

4. Add the cardamom, cinnamon, chili, and stock to the saucepan and bring to a simmer over high heat. Reduce the heat to medium-low and cook, uncovered, for 20 to 25 minutes, or until the pumpkin cubes begin to dissolve in the liquid.

5. Remove the cinnamon sticks and cardamom pods (if used) and discard. Working in batches if necessary, transfer the soup to a blender or food processor and process until smooth.

6. Return the blended soup to the saucepan and stir in the sliced sage leaves. Season to taste with salt and pepper. Cover to keep warm.

7. In a small saucepan or sauté pan, heat the remaining ¼ cup grapeseed oil until very hot (it should be about 350°F). Add the whole sage leaves and fry for about 1 minute, or until crisp. Using tongs, gently remove them from the oil and drain on paper towels. Sprinkle lightly with salt and pepper.

8. Reheat the soup gently if necessary. It should be piping hot when served. Ladle into 6 warmed soup bowls and garnish with the crispy sage leaves. Serve at once.

ASPARAGUS, MUSHROOM, and SPRING ONION SOUP

SERVES 8

AS A GARDENER, I OFTEN FIND MYSELF WORKING THE SOIL DURING THE COLD, blustery days of early spring, and the idea of this warm, rich soup waiting for me in the kitchen keeps me going. Making soup with two of spring's most reliable harbingers, asparagus and mushrooms, makes infinite sense. We often see these two vegetables paired in restaurants, but rarely find them together in a soup. As for body, there is nothing light about this soup, yet it tastes fresh and hopeful, just like springtime. With the first asparagus in the markets and the garden, it's time to move beyond winter's root vegetables and joyfully enter the new season. Mushrooms, too, are typical spring products and are sure signs that better days are just around the corner. Both fight off the winter blues, and while both are available for months to come, I especially appreciate their connection to early spring.

This thick, warm soup is not bright green, like spring pea soup, for instance, but is instead more of a pistachio color. The amazing earthy flavor makes the kind of great seasonal statement that I love. Early spring onions add both dimension and bright flavor, and, in case you wondering, are the same thing as scallions or green onions. I like the way the term resonates in the title of this recipe—rings the springtime bell, if you will!

1 POUND CREMINI OR SHIITAKE MUSHROOMS

3 POUNDS ASPARAGUS

4 CUPS WATER

2 TABLESPOONS RICE OIL OR GRAPESEED OIL

2 SCALLIONS, white and green parts thinly sliced and kept separate

14 FRESH SAGE LEAVES

4 TABLESPOONS CLABBERED CREAM (see Note) or crème fraîche

SALT AND FRESHLY GROUND BLACK PEPPER

1. Trim the stems from the mushrooms and put the stems in a medium-large saucepan. Slice the mushroom caps thinly and set aside. Trim the tough ends from the asparagus spears and, using a vegetable peeler, peel the spears to within about 1 inch of the tips. Add the trimmings to the pan holding the mushroom stems.

2. Pour the water into the saucepan and bring to a boil over high heat. Reduce the heat to low and simmer for about 20 minutes.

3. Choose 16 of the best-looking asparagus spears, selecting fairly thin ones, to be used later for garnish. Add the 16 asparagus spears to the saucepan with the reserved peelings and simmer for 1 to 2 minutes to blanch. With tongs or a slotted spoon, lift the spears from the water and immediately immerse in ice water to shock and stop the cooking. Lift the spears from the ice water, drain, and reserve. Strain the cooking broth through a fine-mesh sieve and reserve. Discard the contents of the sieve.

4. Thinly slice the remaining uncooked asparagus spears. Heat a large non-stick skillet over medium heat. When hot, add the oil and heat gently. Add the white parts of the scallions and sauté for 2 to 3 minutes, or soft and translucent. Add the sliced mushroom caps and sauté for 3 to 4 minutes, or until they soften. Add the sliced asparagus, cover partially, and cook for 4 to 6 minutes, or until the asparagus turns bright green. Add the strained broth, bring to a simmer, re-cover partially, and cook for 6 to 8 minutes, or until the flavors blend.

5. Meanwhile, finely slice 6 of the sage leaves (you will have about 1 tablespoon) and keep 8 whole.

6. Working in batches if necessary, transfer the soup to a blender or food processor and process until smooth. Return the puréed soup to the pan. Stir in 2 tablespoons of the cream and the cut sage leaves. Season to taste with salt and pepper. Reheat gently, if necessary, but do not allow the soup to boil.

7. Ladle the soup into 8 warmed soup bowls. Garnish each bowl with a whole sage leaf, sliced scallion greens, 2 of the blanched asparagus spears, and a dollop of the remaining 2 tablespoons cream, divided equally. Serve at once.

NOTE: Clabbered cream is thick, slightly curdled milk, sometimes called thick milk. See the Glossary (page 219) for more information.

Chilled
GARDEN BERRY SOUP
with Lemon Verbena

SERVES
6

LEMON VERBENA, ONE OF MY FAVORITE HERBS, IS DIFFICULT TO FIND (YOU CAN USUALLY BUY IT AT FARMERS' MARKETS), SO I GROW MY OWN. I am always happy when I walk past it or pick it and get a whiff of its intoxicating, fresh, lemony scent—particularly late on a hot, sunny day when the herb is at its headiest. If you are using seeds, start them in a sunny window in late winter or very early spring and transplant to the garden in mid-May, where the herb will flourish until fall. I advise cutting the verbena back, mulching, and then covering it with straw for over wintering. This is not always successful, but if it is, the hassle is well worth it. Eventually, lemon verbena will turn into a shrublike plant that just keeps on giving! In case the heavy mulching fails (the winter could be extremely harsh, for example), take a few cuttings in late summer, root them in water, and plant in a pot

to hold for spring planting. In mild climates, verbena grows into a small, sprawling tree. I am surprised it's not more popular. This recipe may help spread the word about its magic.

I *love* lemon verbena with fresh berries, and there is no better way to marry the two than in a soup or dessert. I particularly enjoy healthful, refreshing berry soups. The addition of a little salt, hot chili pepper, and lemon juice keeps the soup from tasting like a dessert sauce, while giving it wonderful zip. The base recipe below works for any berry, and you can mix and match other citrus juices and herbs. For instance, I find lime juice and cilantro is just the right choice for blueberry soup—with some additional hot chilies, of course!

continued

chilled garden berry soup
with lemon verbena

continued

I CUP LOCAL HONEY

I CUP FRESH LEMON JUICE

2 TABLESPOONS GRATED LEMON
ZEST

I CINNAMON STICK

4 TO 5 TEASPOONS SEEDED,
FINELY MINCED JALAPEÑO or other
fresh chili (about I small jalapeño)

¼ CUP THINLY SLICED FRESH
LEMON VERBENA STEMS

½ TEASPOON FINE SEA SALT

6 PINTS FAVORITE GARDEN
BERRY IN SEASON such as
strawberry, raspberry, or blueberry

¼ CUP LOOSELY PACKED, SLICED
FRESH LEMON VERBENA LEAVES

1. In a small saucepan, combine the honey, lemon juice, lemon zest, cinnamon stick, 4 teaspoons chili, and verbena stems in a small saucepan over medium-low heat. Bring to a simmer and cook for about 5 minutes, or until the flavors are well developed. If you like a little more zip, add more minced chili. Season with the salt, remove from the heat, and let cool for 10 minutes.

2. Put the berries in a food processor. Pour the honey mixture through a fine-mesh sieve held over the berries and then process until smooth. Adjust the seasoning with salt and lemon juice.

3. Rinse the sieve, and then strain the soup through the sieve into a glass bowl. Skim any foam that rises to the surface. Stir in the sliced verbena leaves, cover, and chill for about 1 hour before serving.

4. Taste and adjust the seasoning before serving in chilled bowls.

RICH CHICKEN SOUP

SERVES
8 TO 10

MAKING THIS CHICKEN SOUP TAKES MORE TIME THAN WORK, but it requires both and both are well worth it. My mother taught me how important it is to have chicken broth (her word for stock) in the house so that I could start a soup anytime I wanted. It's better than using water, she said, and I agree. Still, there are times when I don't have stock on hand, so I developed this recipe for homemade chicken soup.

Begin with free-range, responsibly raised chickens. That means the birds have had the opportunity to exercise their muscles and develop good flavor and minimal fat. They also live longer because the farmers don't pump them full of growth hormones and antibiotics. A chicken raised with these "enhancements" reaches its prime weight of 3½ pounds in six to eight weeks, while a chicken raised the old-fashioned way takes nearly three months to reach the same weight. I guess you could conclude that the saying "Age equals character" applies to more than Humphrey Bogart and Katharine Hepburn! Plus, these chickens have eaten only what nature intended them to eat. I use the plural intentionally, because this recipe calls for two birds. If you already have chicken stock in the freezer, start making the soup when the instructions for the second chicken begin; otherwise, use two and you will end up with a nice, rich soup.

The first chicken is used solely for making the stock that acts as the base for the soup. The second chicken further flavors the soup base, and its meat is added to the soup before serving. But, you might ask, what about the meat from chicken number one? Lori and I and the kids usually just pull it from the bones and eat it while standing around the butcher block island

continued

rich chicken soup

continued

in our kitchen. It also makes wonderful chicken salad and chicken sandwiches. Or, you can toss it into the soup pot and have a really meaty soup.

The key to this soup is to cook the chickens and vegetables whole. Don't cut them up! This way, you can simmer the vegetables longer—and extract lots of good flavor—without running the risk of them falling apart. Don't worry; they will soften enough so that they can easily be broken apart with the serving ladle. Or, you can remove them once they are cooked, cut them up, and return them to the soup.

Although I don't add noodles in this recipe, you can. I suggest cooking them in the stock once the second chicken and the vegetables have been removed. When the noodles are al dente, return the chicken meat and the vegetables to the pot, heat it up, and go for it! Some people like to cook the noodles separately in water and then add them as needed every time they reheat and serve the soup. This keeps the noodles firmer. Personally, I like the way the noodles turn softer and silkier every time I reheat the soup. Finally, I suggest spelt noodles—they taste like the egg noodles you are accustomed to but are far better for you. Look for them in health-food stores or see Sources (page 221) for a mail-order source.

TWO 3- TO 3½-POUND CHICKENS

COARSE SEA SALT AND FRESHLY CRACKED BLACK PEPPER

3 TO 5 SMALL YUKON GOLD POTATOES

3 CELERY RIBS, trimmed

3 SMALL YELLOW ONIONS, peeled but left whole

2 LARGE CARROTS, peeled

1 TURNIP, peeled

1 BUNCH FRESH FLAT-LEAF PARSLEY or other favorite herb, chopped

1. Select a soup pot large enough to hold 1 chicken and the vegetables with at least 4 inches of room at the top of the pot. Place 1 chicken in the pot and add cold water to cover by 1 inch. Bring to a low boil over medium-high heat. Reduce the heat and simmer gently, skimming any foam that rises to the top, for about 1 hour, or until the chicken is tender enough so that meat is easy to pull from the bones. Remove the chicken from the pot with large tongs and a ladle: Insert one side of the tongs through the neck cavity of the chicken and grasp the backbone with the other side of the tongs. Maneuver the large ladle under the tail end of the chicken and lift. Hold the chicken over the pot for a few seconds to allow the liquid in the cavity to drain back into the pot. Set the chicken aside.

2. Season the chicken broth to taste with salt and pepper. Put the second chicken in the pot and add the potatoes, celery, onions, carrots, and turnip. Add water as needed to cover everything in the pot by 1 or 2 inches.

3. Bring to a gentle boil over medium-high heat. Reduce the heat and simmer gently, skimming any foam and fat that rises to the top, for about 1 hour, or until the chicken is tender. Add the parsley during the last 10 minutes of cooking.

4. Again using the tongs and ladle, lift the whole chicken from the pot. When cool enough to handle, pull the meat from the bones, pull off the skin, and return the meat to the soup. Pull the meat from the first chicken and add it to the soup, or save it for salads and sandwiches. Discard the chicken skin and bones.

5. You can leave the vegetables whole, or remove them with a slotted spoon, cut them up, and return them to the soup. Reheat the soup, if necessary. Taste and adjust the seasoning with salt and pepper. Serve immediately.

SWEET PEA SOUP
with Caramelized Paneer

SERVES **4**
AS A FIRST COURSE

I HAVE SPENT QUITE A LOT OF TIME IN INDIA OVER THE PAST FEW YEARS and have come to love the food and cooking styles of that amazing country. I particularly appreciate how Indian cooks blend sweet and spicy flavors for a flavor experience that almost sneaks up on you—something I first encountered in the Indian state of Gujarat. Some 65 percent of the Indian population are vegetarians, and most of them eat some dairy, which is why I have included paneer, the fresh buffalo's milk cheese found throughout India, in this recipe.

How could I write a book about my garden and leave out a fresh pea soup? English peas, which are familiar to most of us, are grown everywhere, from India to Great Britain to my little ol' state of Connecticut. This soup is a great way to get the full flavor of the fresh peas without puréeing them. They are bold enough to stand up to the other flavors in the soup, including the three classic ingredients from India: paneer, jaggery, and masala spice. This trio provides texture, sweetness, and spiciness, and I promise that once you discover them, you won't turn back. See the Glossary (page 219) for full descriptions of them. I also call for Madras onions, which I discovered in India, too—small, sweet onions very like our red pearl onions. If you can find them, try them. Also, if you need to shell the peas yourself, know that 1 pound of peas in the shell yield about 1 cup of shelled peas.

continued

**8 MADRAS OR RED PEARL
ONIONS, OR SMALL SHALLOTS,**
unpeeled

I TABLESPOON GRAPESEED OIL

**2½ POUNDS SHELLED ENGLISH
PEAS** (about 10 cups)

I RIPE PEAR

**2 OUNCES PANEER OR
BUFFALO MOZZARELLA CHEESE,**
cut into 4 diamond-shaped pieces each
about 1 by 1½ inches

2 TEASPOONS CHAAT MASALA

**¼ TO ½ TEASPOON
HIGH-QUALITY CHILI POWDER**

**3 OUNCES JAGGERY OR LIGHT
BROWN SUGAR,** moistened with
¼ to ½ teaspoon water (about ⅓ cup
firmly packed)

**SALT AND FRESHLY GROUND
BLACK PEPPER**

I. Preheat the oven to 400°F.

2. Toss the onions with the oil and spread on a lightly oiled rimmed baking sheet. Roast for 8 to 10 minutes, or until softened. Transfer to a bowl and, when cool enough to handle, push or pop the onions from the skins. Reserve the onions.

3. Juice the English peas in a heavy-duty juicer. Remove the pulp from the juicer, wrap it in cheesecloth, and, holding it over the pea juice, squeeze it to extract as much juice as possible. This is an important step to get enough juice. You should have about 2 cups. If you don't have a full 2 cups, add water to fill the measure.

4. Quarter the pear and juice the quarters. When you add the pear juice to the pea juice, you will have 2½ to 3 cups juice.

5. In a nonreactive saucepan, heat the combined juices over low heat, stirring gently and constantly, for 3 to 4 minutes, or until the soup thickens and reaches a simmer. Cover to keep warm.

6. Meanwhile, preheat the broiler. Adjust the rack as close to the heat source as possible.

7. Arrange the paneer and onions on a broiler tray.

8. Spread the chaat masala and chili powder in a dry, nonstick skillet, place over medium heat, and toast, shaking the pan gently, for about 1 minute, or until fragrant.

9. Pour the toasted spices into a bowl and add the jaggery. Stir well and then spoon the mixture over the paneer and onions. Broil for 2 to 3 minutes, or until the jaggery caramelizes.

IO. To serve, put a piece of caramelized paneer in the center of each of 4 warmed soup bowls. Set 2 onions beside each piece of paneer. Reheat the soup gently until hot, if necessary. Ladle soup into each bowl, leaving the top of the paneer exposed. Serve immediately.

Heirloom BEAN and TOMATO SOUP

SERVES
6

MANY HOME GARDENERS' HEARTS BREAK WHEN THEY SEE AN OVERRIPE TOMATO THAT HAS FALLEN TO THE GROUND AND SPLIT. Don't despair! Follow me while I show you how to use your noble fallen soldiers in this rich, full-bodied soup. They are also good for sauces and stews.

For the beans, I use tepary beans, a Native American bean indigenous to the Southwest. Terrol Dew Johnson, director of the Tohono O'odham, a Native American cultural rejuvenation initiative, says, "The stars are tepary beans and in each bean is the story and lineage of our ancestors."

I CUP DRIED TEPARY, CRANBERRY, APPALOOSA, OR KIDNEY BEANS, soaked in cold water to cover for 2 hours

4 CUPS HAM HOCK STOCK (page 56)

I TEASPOON FINE SEA SALT

2 TABLESPOONS GRAPESEED OR RICE OIL

I YELLOW ONION, cut into ¼-inch-thick slices

3 LARGE, OVERRIPE TOMATOES, cored and cut into large cubes

I FRESH SAGE SPRIG

FRESHLY GROUND BLACK PEPPER

---

1. Drain and rinse the beans. Put them in a large stockpot and add the stock. Bring to a boil over high heat and immediately reduce the heat to a simmer. Cook gently, skimming any foam that rises to the top, for about 1 hour, or just until tender. When the beans are done, stir in the salt. This will stop the cooking.

2. Heat a large sauté pan over medium heat. When hot, add the oil and then immediately add the onion. Sauté, stirring, for about 5 minutes, or until softened. Add the tomatoes, toss with the onion, and cook for about 1 minute, or until the tomatoes begin to soften. Transfer the tomatoes and onion to the pot with the beans.

3. Add the sage to the soup, bring to a simmer, and cook for 2 to 3 minutes, until the flavors blend and the tomatoes break down. Adjust the seasoning with salt and pepper. Ladle into warmed soup bowls and serve at once.

NOTE: To transform this soup into a main-course stew, start with 1½ cups beans and 4 large tomatoes.

HAM HOCK STOCK

MAKES
ABOUT **2** QUARTS

THIS STOCK MAY NOT SOUND HEALTHFUL BUT, AS WITH ANY STOCK, CAREFUL SKIMMING IS KEY TO MAKING IT AS FAT FREE AS POSSIBLE. Although attending to skimming is important for every stock, it is especially essential for this one. Ham hocks give off more foam and fat than other bones, which means it's necessary to skim constantly. If you feel this might be more trouble—or more boring—than it's worth, don't despair. Stock made from ham hocks is the best smelling and richest tasting of all, so enjoy the aroma while you skim!

5 POUNDS FRESH HAM HOCKS

5 POUNDS SMOKED HAM HOCKS

I. Put all the hocks in a stockpot large enough to hold them with at least 6 inches of room at the top of the pot. You may need 2 pots. Add cold water to cover the hocks by 1 inch. Bring to a full simmer over medium heat. Skim off the foam that forms on the surface. It's important to keep the foam from simmering back into the stock, which will make it cloudy.

2. Reduce the heat to medium-low and cook, uncovered, at a very low simmer for 5 hours, continuing to skim the foam and fat from the stock.

3. Remove from the heat and let the stock cool nearly to room temperature. This allows the hock meat to adhere better to the bone, making it easier to strain the stock without bits of meat escaping through the sieve.

4. Using tongs, lift out the hocks and set aside. Reserve the meat for another use or discard. Strain the stock through a fine-mesh sieve into a bowl. Now line the sieve with 3 layers of dampened cheesecloth and strain the stock a second time. Measure the stock and pour into a clean saucepan. You should have about 4 quarts.

5. Place the stock over medium-high heat, bring to a boil, and boil, uncovered, for about 45 minutes, or until reduced by half. Remove from the heat and plunge the pot into a sink filled halfway with water and ice to cool. Pour into 1 or more storage containers, cover, and refrigerate for up to 3 days or freeze for up to 2 months.

Simple
VEGETABLE STOCK

MAKES
ABOUT **2** QUARTS

IT IS IMPORTANT TO BE ABLE TO MAKE A GOOD VEGETABLE STOCK FOR THOSE OCCASIONS WHEN YOU WANT A PARTICULARLY LIGHT FLAVOR or when a vegetarian soup or other dish calling for stock is on the menu. This recipe is so simple that once you get all the ingredients in the pot, you can turn to other tasks, and all the ingredients are easily grown in the garden.

I CUP CHOPPED YELLOW ONION

I CUP CHOPPED, PEELED TURNIP

⅔ CUP CHOPPED CELERY

I CUP CHOPPED, PEELED CARROT

⅔ CUP CHOPPED FENNEL

⅔ CUP CHOPPED PARSLEY ROOT or stems

I. Combine all the ingredients in a stockpot large enough to hold them with at least 6 inches of room at the top of the pot. Add cold water to cover by 1 inch.

2. Bring to a full simmer over medium heat and simmer, uncovered, for 2 hours. Strain through a fine-mesh sieve, pressing on the vegetables with the back of a large spoon to force out as much of the liquid as possible. Now line the sieve with 3 layers of dampened cheesecloth and strain a second time. Let cool, pour into 1 or more storage containers, cover, and refrigerate for up to 1 week or freeze for up to 1 month.

Rich
CHICKEN STOCK

MAKES ABOUT
4
CUPS

NOTE THAT THERE IS ONLY ONE INGREDIENT IN THIS STOCK, other than water. I like the pure flavor of chicken and cool, clear water. (Use filtered water if you can.) This way, the final essence is just chicken and not muddied with competing flavors of vegetables or herbs. I follow the same philosophy when making all meat stocks—just bones and water. I suggest you buy bone-in chickens and bone them yourself. Store the bones in the freezer and use them to make stock. The bony chicken parts sold for stock tend to be fatty.

5 POUNDS CHICKEN BONES AND BONY CHICKEN PARTS, trimmed of excess fat

1. Preheat the oven to 425°F.

2. Put the bones and bony parts in 2 large roasting pans or deep baking pans. Do not crowd them in the pans. Roast, turning the bones and parts several times, for about 45 minutes, or until well browned.

3. Transfer the chicken bones and parts to a stockpot large enough to hold them with at least 6 inches of room at the top of the pot. Add cold water to cover by 1 inch. Bring to a full simmer over medium heat. Scoop about 2 cups of the simmering water from the pot and pour about 1 cup into each of the roasting pans. Swirl the water in the pans, stirring to scrape up the browned bits from the bottom of each pan, and return the water to the pot.

4. Skim off the foam that forms on the surface. It's important to keep the foam from simmering back into the stock, which will make it cloudy.

5. Reduce the heat to medium-low and cook, uncovered, for 2½ hours, continuing to skim the foam and fat from the stock.

6. Using tongs or 2 spoons, lift out the chicken bones and parts and set aside. Strain the stock through a fine-mesh sieve into a bowl. Now line the sieve with a 3 layers of dampened cheesecloth and strain the stock a second time. Measure the stock and pour into a clean saucepan. You should have about 2 quarts.

7. Place the stock over medium-high heat, bring to a boil, and boil, uncovered, for about 30 minutes, or until reduced by half. Remove from the heat and plunge the pot into a sink filled halfway with water and ice to cool. Pour into a storage container, cover, and refrigerate for up to 3 days or freeze for up to 2 months.

THE BENEFITS AND CARE OF CAST-IRON COOKWARE

Cast-iron pans heat more slowly than other pans, but once hot, they hold their heat uniformly and efficiently for a good, long time. This makes them favorite pans of mine—particularly cast-iron skillets. I cook food in cast iron in several recipes in the book, often relying on two hot pans to sandwich the food so that it cooks from both sides or simply using the top pan to weight the food. It's a useful technique you will come to love.

To heat cast-iron pans, even before you put any food in them (including oil), set them on high heat and let them heat up for 4 or 5 minutes. When they start to smoke, reduce the heat a little but leave them alone for at least 4 full minutes. This ensures they will be perfectly hot and ready for cooking.

To season a new pan, first get it very hot on the stove top. Then pour some vegetable oil into it and, using a large wad of paper towels, rub a layer of oil over the interior of the hot pan. Let the pan cool before using it.

Cast-iron pans are heavy, no denying, but if you can wield a spade and hoe in the garden, you can heft a cast-iron pan. They can't go in the dishwasher and must be dried as soon as they are washed or they will rust. However, you will learn to live with these two drawbacks to modern living. Here's a trick: Wash the pans with warm, soapy water, rinse well, and then set on a back burner over medium heat while you finish tidying up the kitchen. In a matter of minutes the pans will be dry. Turn off the flame and let the pans cool.

main courses

ONE OF THE REASONS LORI AND I ARE SO DEDICATED TO GARDENING IS THAT IT ALLOWS US TO AFFORD TO BUY RESPONSIBLY RAISED MEAT AND POULTRY AND WILD-CAUGHT FISH. When I decide what to cook, I like to make choices that have positive effects on farming communities, the environment, and the health of my family. It's important to realize the choices we make have a direct impact on our health and the health of our planet. And of course, the food must taste good.

In the note preceding the recipe for GRILLED FRESH SARDINES WITH SUMMER TOMATOES AND LEMON on page 74, I talk about the choices you can make when buying seafood. Similar arguments can be made when buying poultry and meat. I avoid the supermarket meat counter and turn instead to smaller markets and butchers where I know the sources of what they sell. You can also order responsibly raised meat and poultry by mail; turn to page 221 for more information.

I like to work with farmers such as Paul Willis of Thornton, Iowa, who raises hogs for Niman Ranch, a beef and pork producer committed to humane animal husbandry and sustainable ranching practices. Bill Niman and his network of producers raise hogs and beef cattle naturally, without the use of hormones or antibiotics. I've been to Paul's farm and have seen the pigs in fields and the sows in their hoop houses suckling their piglets. The air is full of the sweet smells of a well-managed pasture pork farm and the contented squeaks and grunts of happy pigs and piglets.

It's vital to understand that we take lives to move our own lives forward; we cannot ignore this reality.

When I was a kid, I remember a pig named Roy on my grandfather's farm in Morley, Missouri. When it was time to eat Roy, my mom reminded us to think of the hog as we dug into Sunday dinner. I was sad, but I also recall thinking how good Roy tasted. All this explains why I feel so strongly about raising animals humanely and in stress-free environments. Nature intended for species to treat one another with common sense and dignity. When we follow nature's lead, she rewards us with great flavor. Responsibly raised, properly fed, and humanely terminated animals taste remarkably better than conventionally raised animals. In fact, credible national newspapers and magazines, such as the *New York Times* and *Bon Appétit,* have conducted taste tests that support this statement!

In this chapter, I have only one recipe for beef. I love beef but believe it should be eaten less frequently than other forms of protein. I focus more emphasis on recipes for lamb, pork, and chicken. For good health, we should take more of our nonfish protein from these meats, which is not to say that eating beef is not healthful. Beef contains many essential nutrients, such as vitamin B_{12}, zinc, and iron, but it's more difficult to digest than other protein sources and is also high in saturated fat. The point is that all protein groups play an important role in an exciting and diverse meal plan. The key is variety and to strike the right balance of protein to complex carbohydrate.

WILD-CAUGHT SALMON SATAY
with Asian-Style Pesto

**SERVES
4**

WILD-CAUGHT SALMON IS THE DARLING OF CHEFS, but don't think of it as a fad or an elite chef thing. Not only is it more flavorful than its farm-raised cousin, but it is also packed with a higher percentage of omega-3 fatty acids. Another important reason for seeking it out is that wild salmon fishing is more environmentally friendly than the production of farm-raised salmon and it employs fishermen. Sure, the wild fish is more expensive and you may not always be able to find it, but when you can, use it. If your fishmonger does not carry wild salmon, ask if he or she can order it for you.

I personally believe we should adjust our portion plan to eat smaller portions of protein and larger portions of fresh vegetables. Instead of eight ounces of salmon and four ounces of vegetables, I recommend four to five ounces of salmon and eight ounces of veggies.

Add a side dish such as SKILLET-BROWNED BROCCOLI AND CAULIFLOWER WITH PAN-TOASTED GARLIC (page 125), and you have a health-and-flavor powerhouse that combines protein, fiber, omega-3 fatty acids, and complex carbohydrates.

The pesto I spread on the salmon is quite different from classic Mediterranean pesto. First, there's not a basil leaf in sight, nor is there Parmesan cheese or pine nuts. I believe pesto is more of a concept than a specific recipe and lends itself to a variety of culturally based preparations. I use mint, cilantro, and parsley, as well as garlic and a little spicy jalapeño. If you're gardening with herbs, you need ways to use them. Here's a terrific one!

continued

PESTO

3 CLOVES GARLIC, smashed

¼ TO ½ GREEN JALAPEÑO CHILI,
seeded and chopped

**¾ CUP LOOSELY PACKED
FRESH CILANTRO LEAVES**

**¼ CUP LOOSELY PACKED
FRESH MINT LEAVES**

**¼ CUP LOOSELY PACKED FRESH
FLAT-LEAF PARSLEY LEAVES**

**2 TABLESPOONS THINLY SHAVED
FRESH LEMONGRASS** (optional)

**I TABLESPOON GRAPESEED
OR CANOLA OIL**

**2 TEASPOONS GRATED
FRESH GINGER**

½ TEASPOON ASIAN SESAME OIL

JUICE OF 2 LIMES

SALT

**ONE 18-OUNCE SKINLESS
SALMON FILLET**

**2 TEASPOONS GRAPESEED
OR CANOLA OIL**, plus more for brushing

**I TABLESPOON FINELY MINCED
YELLOW ONION**

¾ CUP LONG-GRAIN BROWN RICE

I½ CUPS RICH CHICKEN STOCK
(page 58), heated

**2 TEASPOONS BLACK OR
WHITE SESAME SEEDS**, toasted

**4 FRESH SPRIGS EACH MINT,
CILANTRO, AND FLAT-LEAF PARSLEY**

I. To make the pesto, in a mini processor, combine the garlic, jalapeño, cilantro, mint, parsley, lemongrass (if using), grapeseed oil, ginger, and sesame oil. Process until smooth. Season to taste with lime juice and salt and set aside.

2. Lay the salmon fillet flat on a cutting surface so the thinnest pointed part of the fillet faces you. Cut it in half from top to bottom. Cut each half in half, again cutting from top to bottom. Continue cutting the salmon this way until you have 12 equal slices.

3. Lay the slices on the cutting surface, flat side down, and insert a 6-inch bamboo skewer into each slice, threading it through the salmon strips so that the strips are impaled on the skewers. The salmon skewers should resemble a rectangular lollipop. Brush the pesto on all sides of the salmon. Lay a piece of plastic wrap lengthwise over a cutting board. Arrange the skewers vertically side by side on the plastic wrap, with the salmon at the center of the wrap and the skewers pointing down and away from the wrap. Fold the upper half of the wrap over the salmon and transfer to a baking sheet large enough to hold all the skewers. Refrigerate.

4. In a medium saucepan, heat the 2 teaspoons oil over medium-high heat just until it begins to ripple. (The ripples mean it is hot.) Add the onion and sauté for about 1 minute, or until translucent. Add the brown rice and stir until well combined with the onion. Add the stock. Because it's already warm, it will begin to simmer almost immediately. Stir once, reduce the heat to low, cover tightly, and cook for 45 minutes, or until the rice has absorbed the liquid and is tender. Remove the rice from the heat and set aside, covered, for 10 minutes.

5. While the rice is resting, heat a nonstick griddle pan or large sauté pan over medium-high heat until hot. Unwrap the skewered salmon pieces and lightly brush the salmon with oil. Place the salmon in the hot pan and cook, turning once, for about 2 minutes on each side, or until browned.

6. To serve, lightly oil four 3-ounce ramekins or custard cups and sprinkle ½ teaspoon of the sesame seeds over the bottom of each. Carefully fill each ramekin with rice and pack lightly. Invert each ramekin onto a warmed plate, and then lift off the ramekin to reveal a nicely molded rice mound. Rest 3 salmon skewers against the rice, and garnish each plate with the mint, cilantro, and parsley sprigs.

Dry-Rubbed Grilled Fillet of
SALMON

SERVES
6

CILANTRO, ALSO KNOWN AS CORIANDER, grows well in any sized garden, from a large plot to a small window box. If you start with seeds, you can grow the herb year-round because it flourishes indoors, too. Outdoors, you may have to reseed once or twice after midsummer because it will bolt early—but this is not a chore.

This recipe is designed for cilantro lovers. It uses a lot of the herb, so if you don't particularly like its flavor, pick something different, such as basil. This recipe is also a good way to introduce cilantro and salmon to each other. Salmon is a fish from northern waters, but it nonetheless loves the warm, sunny flavors of the Southwest, where cilantro plays a large role. The cumin and chili powder combine with the cilantro to evoke these flavors, and the result is a fish that tastes just great with salsa, especially if the salsa is made with garden-ripe tomatoes. Be sure to use pure chili powder, rather than a compound powder (see the Glossary, page 219, for more information), for the best result. Use this same rub with chicken, flank steak, ribs, or pork—but don't forget about the salmon. The rub caramelizes quickly on the fish and clings to it with wonderful flavor.

continued

dry-rubbed grilled fillet of salmon

continued

I CUP RAW CANE SUGAR

1¼ CUPS CHOPPED FRESH CILANTRO

½ CUP GRATED LIME ZEST

½ CUP PLUS I TABLESPOON COARSE SEA SALT

¼ CUP PLUS 2 TABLESPOONS CHILI POWDER

¼ CUP PLUS 2 TABLESPOONS GROUND CUMIN

3 POUNDS SKINLESS WILD-CAUGHT SALMON FILLETS, about 1½ inches thick at the thickest part

I. In a bowl, combine the sugar, 1 cup of the cilantro, the lime zest, the ½ cup salt, the ¼ cup chili powder, and the ¼ cup cumin. Mix well.

2. Lay a sheet of parchment paper over a baking sheet large enough to hold the salmon fillets. Spread half the dry rub over an area of the paper about the size of the fillets. Lay the fillets on top of the rub. Sprinkle the remaining dry rub over the top of the salmon and pat gently.

3. Let the salmon sit at room temperature for 1 hour or in the refrigerator for 2 hours. As it sits, the rub will draw moisture from the fish and become wet. It is at this point that the rub begins to cure the salmon.

4. Meanwhile, in a small bowl, combine the remaining 2 tablespoons each chili powder and cumin and 1 tablespoon salt and mix well.

5. Prepare a charcoal or gas grill for grilling over a medium-hot fire. If using charcoal, mound the coals to one side of the grill for indirect grilling. If using a gas grill, turn one of the burners to low. Rub the grill rack with a cloth saturated with a good amount of vegetable oil and set the rack over the hot coals.

6. Using a large, sharp knife, thoroughly scrape the dry rub from the salmon and discard the rub. Using your fingers, rub the newly mixed batch of rub into both sides of the fish.

7. Place the salmon on the grill rack over the hottest part of the fire and grill, turning once, for 1 to 2 minutes on each side, or until the fish is well marked with grill marks. Watch the fillets carefully, since the sugar in the dry rub will caramelize.

8. Move the salmon to the cooler part of the grill and cook for 10 to 12 minutes longer, or until the fish reaches an internal temperature of 145°F. Serve immediately, garnished with the remaining ¼ cup cilantro.

CRISPY STRIPED BASS
with Tomato and Onion Sauce

**SERVES
6**

I SUSPECT THAT MORE GARDENERS GROW TOMATOES THAN ANY OTHER PLANT, whether they are raising a variety of heirlooms on a large patch of ground or cherry tomatoes in a patio pot. If you take care of the plants, making sure they get enough sunshine and regular watering and staking them when they grow tall, you will get a good crop. Nothing beats a sun-ripened tomato, plucked from the vine.

For this recipe, I cook the tomatoes very quickly. They are ready when they reach a saucy consistency that is still chunky with a viscosity that clings to the fish. This recipe employs one of my favorite techniques: I use a second cast-iron skillet to weight the fish for a few moments during cooking. Striped bass, also known as stripers, should not be hard to find. But if you have trouble, the sauce can be served with grilled sardines; roast cod; or salmon.

I take the time to squeeze the seeds from the tomatoes first and then chop the flesh.

Seeds, juice, and flesh are all cooked together in a hot pan with a little butter and onion, but I find the sauce comes together more satisfactorily if tomatoes are prepped this way. I don't season the sauce with the herbs until it's off the heat, so that their flavors stand out. Marjoram and oregano are great herbs with tomatoes, but you can use whatever you like best or whatever is most abundant in the garden.

If you grow tomatoes, you know that it's common to have fallen, cracked, or overripe tomatoes, and these are the ones I most often use for sauce. The advanced ripeness means they are tangier and thus perfect for short cooking, which also brings out their natural sweetness. I call for Red Barrel onions here, which look like bulbous scallions with a reddish hue. If you see them, grab them. Can't find them? Use large scallions instead.

continued

4 RIPE HEIRLOOM TOMATOES
(about 1½ pounds total)

SIX 6-OUNCE STRIPED BASS,
white bass, or red snapper fillets, skin on

**2 TABLESPOONS RICE OR
GRAPESEED OIL**

**SALT AND FRESHLY GROUND
BLACK PEPPER**

3 RED BARREL ONIONS or scallions,
trimmed and the entire onion halved lengthwise, **PLUS 4 RED BARREL ONIONS**
or scallions, white and green parts, sliced
vertically

¼ CUP EXTRA-VIRGIN OLIVE OIL

**2 TABLESPOONS COLD UNSALTED
BUTTER**

**¼ CUP THINLY SLICED FRESH
CHIVES**

**2 TABLESPOONS FRESH MARJORAM
OR OREGANO LEAVES**

1. Core the tomatoes and cut in half through the equator. Hold the tomato halves over a glass bowl and squeeze gently to remove the seeds and juice. Reserve the juice and seeds. Finely chop the tomato halves with a sharp knife, add to the bowl with the seeds and juice, and set aside. You will have about 2 cups.

2. Have ready 2 large cast-iron skillets, each one large enough to hold the fish fillets in a single layer. Heat 1 cast-iron skillet over medium heat until hot. Rub both sides of each fish fillet with rice oil and season both sides with salt and pepper. Put the fillets, skin side down, in the hot skillet. Put the second skillet on top of the bass to weight the fillets so that the skin crisps evenly. Cook for 3 to 4 minutes, rotating the bottom pan by quarter turns every 50 to 60 seconds to ensure the skin crisps evenly. Remove the top pan, turn the fillets over, and cook, without the top pan, for 2 to 4 minutes longer, or until the fillets are just cooked through. The timing will depend on the thickness of the fillets.

3. While the fish cooks, lay the 3 split onions on the side of the pan, right along the edge (the crotch of the pan), and cook alongside the fish for the final 2 minutes or so of cooking. Remove from the pan and set aside to use for garnish.

4. Transfer the fillets, skin side up, to a large warmed platter.

5. Add the olive oil and the 4 sliced onions to the pan over medium heat and sauté for about 1 minute, or until soft and translucent. Add the reserved tomato seeds, juice, and chopped tomatoes and the butter and simmer with strength for about 2 minutes, or until thickened and saucy.

6. Remove the skillet from the heat and stir in the chives and marjoram. Season to taste with salt and pepper.

7. Arrange the fillets on 6 warmed plates or leave them on the platter. Top with the sauce and garnish with the pan-seared onions. Serve immediately.

SEARED SEA SCALLOPS
with Spring-Dug Parsnip Butter

SERVES
4

SO MANY GARDENERS, WHETHER THEY ARE BACKYARD HOBBYISTS OR SMALL FARMERS WHO GROW PRIMARILY FOR GREEN MARKETS, are frustrated in the spring because of the lack of green vegetables. But there are a few items in the garden that are exciting to use and this recipe makes good use of two wonderful natural treasures: spring-dug parsnips and chervil.

A good friend, chef Peter Davis of Henrietta's Table in Cambridge, Massachusetts, introduced me to spring-dug parsnips from nearby Verrill Farms. It's a perennial root in northern regions, and when properly tended, survives the winter so that it can be dug in the spring when fresh greens begin to appear on the tops. The root benefits from parboiling and then roasting to bring out its overwintered sweetness. When it is puréed, its texture is similar to very smooth apple butter—yet no butter is involved.

This sweetness goes well with chervil, one of my all-time favorite cool-weather herbs. The marriage of the rich, sweet, earthy parsnips and the mildly licorice-flavored chervil is a surefire hit with sea scallops. Rely on a little lemon juice and zest to cut the sweetness of this pleasing spring dish, which can also be served as a first course for six.

continued

seared sea scallops
with spring-dug parsnip butter

continued

**I LARGE OR 2 MEDIUM
SPRING-DUG PARSNIPS,**
peeled (about IO ounces total)

GRATED ZEST OF I LEMON

JUICE OF ½ LEMON

**I TO 2 TABLESPOONS
EXTRA-VIRGIN OLIVE OIL**

**2 TABLESPOONS FIRMLY PACKED,
CHOPPED FRESH CHERVIL,**
plus 6 generous sprigs for garnish

**SALT AND FRESHLY GROUND
BLACK PEPPER**

2 TABLESPOONS GRAPESEED OIL

I2 LARGE DRY SEA SCALLOPS
(about I2 ounces total) (see Note)

I. Preheat the oven to 375°F. Lightly oil a rimmed baking sheet.

2. In a saucepan, combine the parsnips with water to cover by about 1 inch. Bring to simmer over medium heat and parboil for about 15 minutes. Remove the pan from the heat and set aside to cool slightly. Lift the parsnips from the pan and reserve ¼ cup of the liquid.

3. Slice the parsnip into ½-inch-thick pieces and lay the pieces on the prepared baking sheet. Roast for 20 to 25 minutes, or until nicely browned. Turn the parsnips at least once during roasting to ensure even browning.

4. Transfer the parsnips to a food processor. Add the lemon zest and lemon juice and pulse until the parsnips break down. With the motor running, add the reserved ¼ cup liquid 1 tablespoon at a time and process until the mixture resembles loose peanut butter or apple butter. Finish by slowly pulsing in the olive oil and chopped chervil. Season to taste with salt and pepper. Scrape into a dish or small saucepan with a lid and set aside to keep warm. You should have about 2 cups.

5. Heat a large, dry skillet or sauté pan over high heat. Brush each scallop on all sides with the grapeseed oil and season with salt and pepper. Put the scallops in the hot pan and do not move them for 2 to 3 minutes, or until the edges are well browned. Turn the scallops over and cook for 1 to 2 minutes longer, or until cooked through.

6. Put the scallops on a warmed plate and let them rest for 2 minutes. If juice pools on the plate, stir it into the parsnip purée for extra flavor.

7. Divide the parsnip purée evenly among 4 warmed dinner plates, placing it in the center. Set 3 scallops on top of each mound and garnish with the chervil sprigs. Serve at once.

NOTE: Buy scallops that look creamy white or even slightly pink. These have not been soaked in a preservative solution, which is what turns many commercial scallops bright white. Good fishmongers typically carry dry scallops because of their superior quality.

GRILLED FRESH SARDINES
with Summer Tomatoes and Lemon

SERVES
6

THE WORD IS SPREADING THAT SOME OF OUR FAVORITE FISH ARE IN TROUBLE BECAUSE OF OVERFISHING, and because most folks want to do the right thing, a lot of people ask me how to make responsible seafood choices. This is not as much from a Samaritan standpoint as it is concern about running out of our favorite fish. I understand this completely because I know how powerful a motivator taste is! While I believe in choice, I also understand that overdemand can cause diminishing supply. It's not as though we can manufacture fish (although salmon and shrimp farmers might argue with me about this!).

Many of our favorite fish are so popular that they are dwindling in numbers to the point of extinction. Some people feel this isn't a big deal. They reason that when we run out of one type of fish, we'll find another. But it's much more complicated than that. Others realize the complications but, lacking a degree in marine biology,

don't have the knowledge to wade through the mounting and intricate data that are continually being debated. The situation is thorny. First, many, rather than a few, species are being over-fished. Second, because of how the food chain works, wiping out a certain species causes imbalance, which in turn causes population excesses or depletions that radically cause star-vation or overeating of other species. This imbalance dramatically rocks the boat (no pun intended) of a very complex ecosystem. Third, because so many of us demand to eat fish like we eat steak—in big, thick cuts—fishermen take the adult fish of a species and leave behind no breeding parents. Imagine what would happen if most humans over the age of eleven disap-peared because another species enjoyed collect-ing large humans. Then when they ran out of large humans, they started collecting eight-through eleven-year-olds. You get the point!

This is precisely what is happening to marlin, Chilean bass, and a variety of other fish. Does this mean we should never again eat certain species? Of course not. But it's a good idea to try a wide variety of fish instead of always demanding the same kinds. This will give the more popular fish time to replenish their own stocks and ensure that fish such as the Chilean bass (aka Patagonian toothfish) will always be there to enjoy.

By broadening our selection, we also are ensured of getting a wider variety of nutrients that are beneficial to adults and children alike. Fish are not only good for their omega-3 fatty acids, but also provide an amazing array of other minerals and nutrients that vary among types. Everyone wants to eat more fish for heart health and other benefits, and just as eating a broad range of vegetables can reduce or eliminate the need for vitamin and mineral supplements, so can eating a wide variety of fish.

More so than with other foods, knowing how to cook fish is crucial. Let's face it, it's easier to eat an overcooked burger than to eat a poorly cooked fish. On the other hand, there is no better dining experience than properly cooked fish. The sardine is a species that complies with this fact. Cooked properly, sardines are about as tasty a fish as you can find. Cook them poorly and you probably won't try them again. The following recipe is great because it is simple and nearly foolproof. Salt, spice, tang, and smoke are often the first flavor cues that come to mind when we think about grilling. And sardines, being full-flavored fish, love these flavors. So, go to a good fish shop, ask for some fresh sardines, and fire up the grill. You're in for a damned tasty treat and you'll be giving another species of fish a well-deserved break. If you can't find sardines, ask for Spanish mackerel, snapper blues (small bluefish available in the Northeast), or any fish about the size of sardines, which are less than eight inches long.

Oh, yes, and don't forget the ice-cold white wine and beer!

continued

grilled fresh sardines
with summer tomatoes and lemon

continued

MARINADE

3 LEMONS, cut into ¼-inch-thick slices

1 SMALL YELLOW ONION, sliced

1½ CUPS EXTRA-VIRGIN OLIVE OIL

¼ CUP BALSAMIC VINEGAR

¼ CUP DRY WHITE WINE

1 TABLESPOON FRESHLY GROUND BLACK PEPPER

2 TEASPOONS RED PEPPER FLAKES

4 TO 6 FRESH ROSEMARY SPRIGS

1. To make the marinade, in a large glass or other bowl, whisk together all the marinade ingredients.

2. Arrange the sardines in a single layer in a shallow glass or other nonreactive dish and pour the marinade over them. Cover with plastic wrap and refrigerate for at least 4 hours or up to overnight.

3. Lift the sardines from the marinade and scrape most of the marinade off the fish. Discard the marinade.

4. Sprinkle both sides of each sardine with the sugar and then generously with salt. Lay the fish on a plate or pan and let them stand for about 1 hour at room temperature.

5. Prepare a charcoal or gas grill for grilling over a medium-hot fire.

6. Lightly brush the onion slices with some of the grapeseed oil and season with salt. Place the onion slices over the hottest part of the fire and grill, turning once, for 3 minutes on each side, or until both sides are nicely marked with grill marks and the onions begin to soften. Remove from the grill, separate into individual rings, and set aside.

7. Add more coals to the grill or turn up the heating elements so that the heat is hot in one part of the grill and medium-hot in another.

8. Wipe the excess sugar and salt from the fish with paper towels or a clean kitchen towel, but take care to leave a thin coating on each fish.

9. In a bowl, toss together the lettuce leaves, parsley leaves, chives, and celery leaves. Set aside.

18 FRESH SARDINES,
each 6 to 8 inches long

2 TEASPOONS FINELY GROUND RAW CANE SUGAR (see Note)

FINE SEA SALT

1 RED ONION, cut into 6 slices each ¼ to ½ inch thick

ABOUT 2 TABLESPOONS GRAPESEED OR RICE OIL

1 CUP TORN SMALL LETTUCE LEAVES, beet tops, or radish tops

1 CUP FRESH FLAT-LEAF PARSLEY LEAVES

¾ CUP ½-INCH-LONG FRESH CHIVES

¾ CUP YOUNG CELERY LEAVES OR WATERCRESS LEAVES

12 BAGUETTE SLICES

¼ CUP PLUS 3 TABLESPOONS EXTRA-VIRGIN LEMON OLIVE OIL or extra-virgin olive oil

1 CLOVE GARLIC

2 TABLESPOONS FRESH LEMON JUICE

1 TABLESPOON LOCAL HONEY, warmed

FRESHLY GROUND BLACK PEPPER

4 RIPE TOMATOES, cut into ½-inch-thick slices

10. Brush the sardines lightly on both sides with the grapeseed oil. Place the fish over the hottest part of the fire and grill, turning once, for about 30 seconds on each side, or until nicely marked with grill marks. Take care; the sardines brown quickly. Transfer the sardines to the cooler part of the grill and grill, turning once, for about 2 minutes on each side, or until the skin is crisp and the flesh feels as though it's ready to pull away from the bone. Using a thin fish spatula, gently transfer the sardines to a warmed platter.

11. Lightly brush the baguette slices with 3 tablespoons of the lemon olive oil and grill over the coolest part of the grill for a few minutes on each side until nicely browned. Rub one side of each bread slice with the garlic clove and sprinkle with a little salt. Keep the baguette croutons warm.

12. In a small bowl, whisk together the remaining ¼ cup lemon oil, the lemon juice, and the honey. Drizzle over the salad greens, toss, and season to taste with salt and pepper.

13. Arrange 2 or 3 tomato slices to the high center of each of 6 room-temperature plates. Divide the salad among the plates, placing it on top of the tomatoes. Arrange 3 sardines against the salad on each plate, and drop the grilled onion rings over the plates. Lean 2 croutons against the side of the salad opposite the sardines and serve.

NOTE: If you have only coarse raw cane sugar, grind it in a mortar with a pestle.

BASIL-STEAMED SHRIMP
over Soba Noodles

SHRIMP IS EATEN WIDELY THROUGHOUT ASIA, MOSTLY BECAUSE IT TASTES GOOD and blends winningly with other flavors, but also because it's an excellent source of protein. I match it with Thai basil and soba noodles to celebrate these Eastern influences. Think about it: This recipe calls for shrimp, basil, and noodles but is not Italian! I adore Italian shrimp dishes, such as garlicky scampi or pasta with red sauce and shrimp, but I took a different tack here by including Dashi powder. Also called dashi flakes, or *hom dashi,* it is a mixture of dried bonito flakes, kombur, and seasonings. Try it, you'll love it!

I grow several types of basil in the garden, including Thai basil, a narrow-leaved, green herb with purple flowers. Try it and you'll want to use it in all dishes requiring basil, Asian or not. If you only have sweet basil or opal basil growing in the garden, use it. Fresh basil is good basil!

This recipe requires the extra step of cooking and shocking the soba noodles before they are added to the broth. This keeps the noodles from overcooking when you heat them in the broth. Finally, I like to steam the shrimp in a bamboo steamer, which provides unique flavor. If you don't have a bamboo steamer, a stainless-steel one works just fine.

continued

SALT

**ONE 8-OUNCE PACKAGE DRIED
SOBA NOODLES**

2 SCALLIONS

I ORANGE

I OUNCE FRESH GINGER, (about
2 inches) peeled and thinly sliced

**I SMALL BUNCH FRESH THAI OR
OTHER BASIL**, plus 10 whole leaves and
4 sprigs

16 LARGE SHRIMP,
peeled and deveined

I RED BELL PEPPER, seeded and cut
lengthwise into very thin strips

6 TO 8 SHIITAKE MUSHROOMS,
stems removed and caps thinly sliced

4 CUPS WATER

**2 TABLESPOONS INSTANT DASHI
POWDER** or 2 bouillon cubes

1. Bring a saucepan of lightly salted water to a boil over high heat. Add the noodles and boil for 2 minutes, or until just al dente. Drain the noodles and immediately plunge them into a bowl of ice water to shock and stop the cooking. Drain and set aside.

2. Trim off 1 inch of the green tops of the scallions and discard. Thinly slice the green tops about halfway to the white base and set aside. Cut off the white base and split the base in half lengthwise. Set aside.

3. Using a vegetable peeler, remove only the orange part, or zest, from the skin of the orange, being careful to leave the white pith right beneath it behind. Reserve the orange for another use.

4. Sprinkle the orange zest and ginger slices with salt and rub them between your fingers to work the salt into them.

5. Lay the halved scallion bases and half of the ginger slices and orange zest on the perforated bottom of a bamboo steamer basket to make a "flavor mat" large enough to accommodate all of the shrimp in a single layer.

6. Lay half of the basil bunch over the flavor mat, being sure to leave some of the other components of the mat exposed. Lay the shrimp on top of the mat and top with the remaining ginger, orange zest, and basil bunch.

7. Evenly spread the red pepper strips around the shrimp. Top the pepper strips with the mushrooms.

8. Pour the water into the steamer pan and bring to a simmer over medium heat. Add the dashi powder and simmer until fully dissolved. Put the steamer basket over the simmering base, cover, and steam for about 6 minutes, or until the shrimp turn pink and are just cooked through. Remove the steamer and set aside covered to keep warm.

9. Add the noodles to the simmering broth just long enough to heat them through. Divide the noodles and broth among 4 warmed bowls. Carefully transfer the red pepper strips and mushroom slices to the bowls. In the center of each bowl, arrange 4 shrimp, overlapping them slightly, over the noodles. Discard the flavor mat.

10. Using a sharp knife, thinly slice the 10 basil leaves into julienne. Sprinkle the julienned leaves and the reserved green scallion slices over the broth in each bowl. Nestle a sprig of fresh basil in the center of each bowl and serve.

LOBSTER and SWEET CORN SUCCOTASH

SERVES
6

IT'S NO SECRET THAT LOBSTER AND CORN LOVE EACH OTHER. Visit any lobster pound along the coast of Maine and you will find an ear of corn on the plate with nearly every lobster. I like to romanticize this affinity with one of my favorite theories: Native Americans used lobster, clam, mussel, and oyster shells to enrich the land in which they grew corn, so to this day, shellfish and corn taste right together. This is an excellent example of the hand of man working with nature to make nature even better. I have also observed this with wine making, where beyond managing the vines, the best wines come from vineyards with the least amount of tinkering by overambitious winemakers.

Succotash has been passed down to us from the Native American tribes of the Northeast. Traditionally, it's made with dried corn, dried beans, and winter root vegetables, which come together in a hearty, healthful, and delicious stew. Flying in the face of tradition, I use fresh vegetables for this version.

These days, we grow edamame and lima beans in our gardens or find them at farm stands. And they are fantastic. These flavors together sing the song of summer.

continued

FOUR 1½-POUND LIVE LOBSTERS

20 TO 24 EARS CORN, shucked

2 TABLESPOONS GRAPESEED OIL

½ CUP DICED SWEET ONION
such as Vidalia or Walla Walla

2 CARROTS, peeled and cut into
¼-inch dice (about 1 cup)

¼ CUP RIESLING WINE

½ VANILLA BEAN, split lengthwise,
or ⅛ teaspoon pure vanilla extract

**1 TABLESPOON JULIENNED
LEMON ZEST**

**1 TABLESPOON FRESH
LEMON JUICE**

**2 CUPS FRESH OR FROZEN
SHELLED EDAMAME, FAVA, OR
LIMA BEANS** (about 4 pounds beans
unshelled) (See Note)

**2 TO 3 TABLESPOONS CHOPPED
FRESH TARRAGON LEAVES**

**SALT AND FRESHLY GROUND
BLACK PEPPER**

NOTE: If using fresh fava beans,
peel away the thin skin covering
each bean before cooking (see
the Glossary, page 219).

1. In a large steaming basket set over boiling water in a pot, cook the lobsters for 6 to 8 minutes, or until the shells turn red. Transfer to a platter or large bowl until cool enough to handle.

2. Hold the body with the claws in one hand and the tail in the other. Hold the lobster over a large bowl and twist off the tail. A lot of liquid will spill into the bowl. Next, twist off the claws. Repeat with the other lobsters.

3. Holding each lobster tail over the bowl, remove the tail meat with your fingers or a fork. Repeat with the claws. Let the lobster juice collect in the bowl. (The meat may be slightly undercooked but will cook completely in the succotash.) Slice the tail meat into ½-inch-wide medallions (rounds). Leave the claw meat whole, if possible. Add the meat to the juice and refrigerate until cold. Discard the shells or reserve them for another use (such as broth).

4. Set aside 2 ears corn. Using a large knife, slice the kernels from the remaining ears. Juice the kernels in a heavy-duty juicer. (A paper cup works well to funnel the kernels into the juicer chute.) You should have about 4 cups corn juice.

5. In a nonstick sauté pan large enough to hold the 2 reserved ears corn, heat the grapeseed oil over medium heat. Put the 2 ears in the middle of the pan and cook for about 5 minutes, turning to brown on all sides. Add the onion and carrots so that they surround the corn. Partially cover the pan and cook, turning the corn to brown the kernels further and stirring the onions and carrots or shaking the pan to ensure even cooking, for about 5 minutes longer, or until the kernels are browned. Remove the ears and set aside to cool. When cool, cut the kernels from the cobs.

6. Add the wine to the pan over medium heat, bring to a simmer, and deglaze the pan, stirring to scrape up all the browned bits from the bottom. Simmer for 2 to 3 minutes, or until the pan is nearly dry.

7. Remove the pan from the heat and let cool for 2 minutes. If the sauté pan seems too small to hold all the ingredients for the finished dish, pour the contents of the sauté pan into a saucepan that will accommodate everything. Stir in the corn juice, vanilla, lemon zest, and lemon juice. Add the beans and corn kernels and return the pan to medium heat. Bring to a simmer, stirring constantly, and cook for 3 to 4 minutes, or until the corn juice begins to thicken.

8. Add the reserved lobster meat and juice. Cook over medium heat until the mixture simmers for 3 to 4 minutes. Remove from the heat and let rest for 3 minutes, stirring gently. Stir in the tarragon and season to taste with salt and pepper. Transfer to a warmed serving dish. Serve immediately.

RIB-EYE STEAKS
with Savory Herbs and Roasted Garlic

SERVES
4

ANYONE WHO HAS ROASTED GARLIC KNOWS
HOW SEDUCTIVE IT IS. When you have a bumper
crop—or have just bought some plump, fresh
good-looking heads from the market—roast a
few every time you fire up the grill, even if you
are not eating them at a particular meal. Stored
in a plastic container or bag, they keep easily for
two to three weeks in the refrigerator. Use them
in salads, spreads, and vinaigrettes. This is a
perfect example of using your grilling time wisely.
The same advice applies to bell peppers and
onions. Place two or three on the grill and keep
them in the fridge for a few days to eat with
grilled chicken or hamburgers or to toss with
pasta.

This recipe exposes my soft spot for rib-eye
steak and garlic. When I buy rib eyes, I ask the
butcher to cut them into 14-ounce steaks and to
trim the tail and cap, which I freeze to use later

for stew or for the incredible RANCHERO-STYLE
STEAK AND EGGS (page 188). Just ask a butcher
at your neighborhood butcher shop or even a
butcher at the supermarket to do this for you
and he or she will likely happily oblige. You may
have to special order the steaks, but a day's
planning is usually all you need. When the
steaks are prepared this way, you're grilling the
eye of the rib eye, which is the thickest, most
succulent part. As in other grilling recipes, I use
the entire herb sprig rather than fussing with
pulling off the leaves.

continued

I HEAD GARLIC

**I TEASPOON GRAPESEED
OR CANOLA OIL**

**FOUR IO-OUNCE BONELESS
RIB-EYE STEAKS**, each about
I inch thick, trimmed

½ TEASPOON SALT

**¼ TEASPOON FRESHLY GROUND
BLACK PEPPER**

4 FRESH ROSEMARY SPRIGS,
each 4 to 5 inches long, soaked in cool
water for 5 minutes and drained

**4 FRESH SUMMER SAVORY,
THYME, OR SAGE SPRIGS**,
each 4 to 5 inches long, soaked in cool
water for 5 minutes and drained

I. Peel the papery outer skin from the garlic but leave enough skin attached to hold the cloves together in the head. Soak the garlic head in water to cover for 30 minutes. Drain and set aside to dry for 15 minutes.

2. Prepare a charcoal or gas grill for grilling over a medium-hot fire. Lightly oil the grill grate.

3. Rub the garlic head with the oil and put on the edge of the grill, away from the most intense heat. Grill for about 25 minutes, turning and rolling the head until it begins to soften. Remove from the grill and set aside to cool.

4. When cool enough to handle, peel the garlic cloves and transfer to a fine-mesh sieve. Using a wooden spoon, push the garlic through the sieve into a small bowl, making a paste.

5. Season the steaks with the salt and pepper. Lay the rosemary sprigs on the grill over the hottest part of the fire, spacing them so that 1 steak can be laid on top of each sprig. Put a steak on top of each sprig and grill, turning once, for 3 to 4 minutes on each side for medium-rare. When you turn the steaks, lay the summer savory sprigs on the grill, placing 1 sprig next to each rosemary sprig and putting the steaks on top of them. Transfer the steaks to a warmed platter with a rim to collect any juices that escape from the meat and let rest for about 5 minutes.

6. Pour any accumulated juices into the garlic and mash gently to mix. Serve the steaks with the garlic sauce drizzled over them.

GRILLED LAMB CHOPS
with Home-Dried Tomatoes and Citrus Yogurt

**SERVES
4 TO 6**

MINT IS ONE OF THE FIRST THINGS TO COME UP IN THE GARDEN IN SPRING, and when you pair it with oven-dried tomatoes from last year, you experience the taste of the season to come along with fond, mellow memories of the season gone by. Both are terrific with lamb. Lamb also offers a great opportunity to celebrate the flavors of South Asia and the Near East, as it does here with garam masala (India), ground sumac (Turkey), and yogurt (both). Good-quality organic yogurt is the best choice because it is nice and tangy and alive with healthful cultures.

½ **CUP** OVEN-DRIED TOMATOES (page 161) **OR SUN-DRIED TOMATOES**, coarsely chopped with a knife or kitchen shears

GRATED ZEST OF 2 LEMONS

I TABLESPOON GROUND SUMAC

I½ CUPS ORGANIC PLAIN WHOLE-MILK YOGURT

SALT AND FRESHLY GROUND BLACK PEPPER

TWELVE 6-OUNCE LAMB LOIN CHOPS, each about I inch thick

2 TABLESPOONS GARAM MASALA or raz al hanout (see page 219)

FRESH MINT SPRIGS for garnish

I. In a small bowl, soak the tomatoes in lukewarm water to cover for 30 minutes. Drain well. Gently squeeze the tomatoes dry in a clean, dry kitchen towel.

2. In food processor, combine the tomatoes, lemon zest, sumac, and yogurt and pulse 2 or 3 times until blended but still textured. Season to taste with salt and pepper. Measure out about ½ cup of the mixture. Cover the rest and refrigerate until serving.

3. Spread both sides of each lamb chop with the ½ cup reserved yogurt mixture. Lay the chops in a shallow dish in a single layer, cover, and marinate for about 1 hour at room temperature or up to 4 hours in the refrigerator.

4. Prepare a charcoal or gas grill for grilling over a medium-hot fire. Lightly oil the grill grate.

5. Wipe the excess marinade from each lamb chop. Season both sides of the chops with salt, pepper, and the garam masala.

6. Place the chops over the hottest part of the fire and grill, turning once, for 1 to 2 minutes on each side for medium-rare, or longer for better done chops. Arrange 2 or 3 chops on each plate (depending on the number of servings you plan) and let rest for 5 minutes. Garnish with the mint and serve with the chilled yogurt mixture.

Minted Grilled LAMB CHOPS

SERVES
8

THIS DISH IS ALL ABOUT TAMING THAT UNRULY AND EVER-SPREADING MINT IN THE GARDEN. You can make only so much iced tea, so the challenge is creating and enjoying recipes that use the herb.

That mint and lamb love each other is no secret, but fresh mint can be overpowering. That explains why I cool it down with a little yogurt and, in so doing, provide the perfect balance for the lamb. Lamb and yogurt have married well for centuries in dishes from Europe, North Africa, the Middle East, and South Asia. When used as a marinade, the yogurt provides a wonderful flavor background that adds zest to the lamb, or, for that matter, to any meat.

1½ CUPS ORGANIC PLAIN WHOLE-MILK YOGURT, drained (see Note)

1¼ CUPS LOOSELY PACKED FRESH MINT LEAVES, plus sprigs for garnish

GRATED ZEST AND JUICE OF 2 LEMONS

SALT AND FRESHLY GROUND BLACK PEPPER

24 LAMB LOIN CHOPS, each about 1 inch thick

2 TABLESPOONS MICHEL'S SPICE POWDER (page 175)

1. In a food processor, combine the yogurt, mint leaves, and lemon zest and juice. Pulse 2 or 3 times, or just until blended. Season to taste with salt and pepper.

2. Spread both sides of each lamb chop with about half of the yogurt mixture. Lay the chops in a shallow nonreactive dish in a single layer, cover, and refrigerate for about 1 hour. Cover and refrigerate the remaining yogurt mixture.

3. Prepare a charcoal or gas grill for grilling over a medium-hot fire. Lightly spray the grilling grate with vegetable oil spray.

4. Wipe the excess marinade from each lamb chop. Season both sides of the chops with salt, pepper, and about half of the spice powder.

5. Place the chops over the hottest part of the fire and grill, turning once, for 1 to 2 minutes on each side for medium-rare, or longer for better done chops. Arrange the chops on a warmed large platter and allow to rest for 5 minutes.

6. Sprinkle the remaining spice powder over the chops and garnish with the mint sprigs. Serve with the chilled yogurt mixture.

NOTE: To drain the yogurt, spoon it into a sieve and set it over a bowl to drain for about 30 minutes.

Oregano-Grilled PORK CHOPS

SERVES
4

THE FLAVOR COMBINATION OF ONION, TOMATOES, AND OREGANO is always a hit and it goes beautifully with pork loin chops, a cut that should not be overlooked for summertime grilling when most of us think only of ribs. Nothing could be easier than this dish, but the better the tomatoes and onions, the better the final product will be, which is where the produce from your garden or a local farmers' market comes in. If you make this in the late summer or early fall, try it with a side of wild rice, which makes this meal a perfect bridge from one season to the next. And if you want to make this recipe indoors, try it in a countertop grill, such as the George Foreman grill. Great!

I SMALL RED ONION
cut into ¼-inch-thick slices

GRAPESEED OR CANOLA OIL
in a mister or spray bottle

FOUR 6-OUNCE BONELESS PORK LOIN CHOPS, each about I inch thick

SALT AND FRESHLY GROUND BLACK PEPPER

I BUNCH FRESH OREGANO

4 FIRM BUT RIPE TOMATOES,
cut into ½-inch-thick slices

1. Prepare a charcoal or gas grill for grilling over a medium-hot fire. Lightly oil the grill grate.

2. Lightly spray the onion slices with oil and lay them around the edge of the grill where the heat is not too intense.

3. Season the pork chops on both sides with salt and pepper and place them over the hottest part of the fire. Set aside some of the oregano for garnish and divide the rest in half. Arrange half of the oregano over the pork chops. Cover the grill and cook for about 4 minutes, turning once, until the chops are cooked through.

4. Transfer the chops and the oregano to a baking sheet and keep warm in a low oven.

5. Season the tomato slices on both sides with salt and pepper and lay them on the grill rack over the hottest part of the fire. Turn the onions; they should be nearly done. Put the rest of the oregano over the tomatoes, cover the grill, and cook for about 2 minutes, or until the tomatoes are heated through and so soft they are nearly ready to collapse.

6. Arrange the tomatoes and onions on a warmed platter. Arrange the pork chops, slightly overlapping them shingle fashion, over the tomatoes and onions and garnish with some of the cooked and the reserved uncooked oregano. Serve at once.

KITCHEN STORAGE FOR THE HARVEST

Once you bring your freshly picked vegetables into the kitchen, it is important to store them correctly. Don't trim or wash the vegetables. Shake off any loose dirt, enclose them in perforated plastic bags, and refrigerate. Large items such as squashes and eggplants don't need to be put in plastic bags. They can go directly into the refrigerator's vegetable drawer, which I suggest lining with a folded kitchen towel or a double thickness of paper towel. This will absorb any moisture. Use most fresh vegetables within 3 or 4 days, although some, such as peppers and eggplant will last for up to a week. Sooner is always better than later, except for winter squashes, which last up to 60 days.

While refrigerator storage is good for most of the harvest, don't store tomatoes in the fridge. Let them sit at room temperature in a bowl or colander, and eat them as soon as you can.

Onions do not need refrigeration but should be stored in a cool, dark place. The same is true of white or red and sweet potatoes. Neither should be refrigerated, but the cooler and darker the storage (down to about 45°F) the better. Use new potatoes within 5 days, sweet potatoes within 10 days, and mature white or red potatoes within 2 to 3 weeks.

Stand herb sprigs in a glass of water, like a bouquet, tent the leafy portion with a plastic bag, and refrigerate. They should stay fresh for a good day or two.

GRILLED SMOKED PORK LOIN ROAST
with Grilled Summer Beans

SERVES
6

IF YOU GROW BEANS IN YOUR GARDEN, OR IF YOU'RE DRAWN TO THEIR SHAPES AND COLORS IN FARMERS' MARKETS, you may find yourself looking for new ways to cook them when you get tired of steaming or sautéing. In this recipe, I grill green beans, yellow wax beans, Dragon Tongue beans (flat pods streaked with purple), or purple beans—whatever I have the most of or have just bought from a local farmer—alongside a whole pork loin. The results are nothing short of spectacular. It takes a little dexterity to balance the beans on the grill rack, but with care you can do it. Here's a trick: Arrange the beans side by side along the blade of a flat metal spatula or pancake turner. Slide the beans off the spatula onto the grill so that the length of the beans is perpendicular to the bars on the grill rack.

If your grill has a lid, you can turn it into a smoky roasting chamber perfect for a whole pork loin. Too often we think of grilling relatively thin pieces of meat and fish, but whole roasts love the grill, too. I use aromatic rosemary sprigs to flavor the smoke that swirls around the pork as it cooks, but you could also use wood chips. In either case, keep the rosemary or the chips dripping wet so they will smoke when added to the grill. The smokiness gives this pork loin a deep roasted flavor. It needs constant tending as it cooks, so keep a cooler of your favorite chilled beverage nearby. Your full attention will be rewarded.

6 FRESH ROSEMARY BUNCHES, about twelve 5-inch sprigs per bunch

½ CUP GRAPESEED OIL

¼ CUP FRESH ORANGE JUICE

¼ CUP LOCAL HONEY

¼ CUP GRATED LEMON ZEST

¼ CUP GRATED ORANGE ZEST

¼ CUP CHOPPED FRESH OREGANO

¼ CUP CHOPPED FRESH SAGE

12 CLOVES ROASTED GARLIC, peeled and mashed (see Note)

2 TABLESPOONS COARSELY CRACKED BLACK PEPPER

ONE 2¾- TO 3-POUND BONELESS PORK LOIN ROAST

2 SLICES BACON, roughly chopped

SALT AND FRESHLY GROUND BLACK PEPPER

1½ POUNDS ASSORTED SNAP BEANS such as green beans, yellow wax beans, Dragon Tongue beans, and/or purple beans, in any combination, stems trimmed and any strings removed

1. Put the rosemary bunches in a large bowl and cover with cold water. Soak for at least 2 hours.

2. In a nonreactive dish large enough to hold the pork loin (or in a large zippered plastic bag), combine the oil, orange juice, honey, lemon and orange zests, oregano, sage, garlic, and cracked pepper. Put the pork loin in the dish and turn to coat. Cover and refrigerate for 2 to 4 hours.

3. Prepare a charcoal or gas grill for grilling over a medium-hot fire. If using charcoal, mound the coals to one side of the grill for indirect grilling. If using a gas grill, turn one of the burners to low. Lightly oil the grill grate.

4. Lift the pork loin from the marinade, scraping any excess marinade from the meat back into the dish. Set the pork aside for 15 to 20 minutes to reach room temperature.

5. Meanwhile, spoon the marinade into a saucepan and add the bacon. Bring to a simmer over medium-high heat and cook for about 15 minutes, or until it has reduced to a saucelike consistency. Remove and discard the bacon. Transfer the sauce to a blender and blend until smooth.

6. Separate 6 of the largest sprigs from the rosemary bunches and set aside. Leave the remaining rosemary in the water.

7. Season the pork on all sides with salt and ground pepper. Place the pork over the hottest part of the fire and cook, turning as needed, until the pork is well marked and browned on all sides. This should take about 10 minutes.

8. Remove half of one of the rosemary bunches from the water and lay the sprigs against the coals on the side that will be closest to the meat when it's moved to the cooler part of the grill. If using a gas grill, lay the rosemary directly over the low burner.

continued

grilled smoked pork loin roast
with grilled summer beans

continued

9. Brush the pork loin on all sides with the sauce, move it to the cooler section of the grill, and cover the grill. While the pork loin cooks, keep adding half bunches of the soaked rosemary to the grill, either against the coals or beneath the loin. This requires tending, but the wet rosemary creates a wonderful smoky environment. Let the pork loin cook for about 1 hour (25 to 35 minutes per pound), turning once or twice during grilling, or until an instant-read thermometer registers 150°F when inserted in the center of the loin.

10. Remove the cover from the grill and lay the beans in a single layer next to the pork loin. Lay the reserved 6 rosemary sprigs on top of the beans. With great care, roll the pork loin over the beans so that the fat side faces down, on top of the rosemary and beans. Cook for 10 to 12 minutes, or just until the beans are tender.

11. Transfer the meat to a cutting board and let it rest for 10 minutes before carving. Remove the rosemary from the top of the beans and reserve for garnish. Spread the beans on a warmed platter large enough to hold them and the sliced pork. Slice the pork and arrange the slices on top of the beans. Garnish with the reserved rosemary.

NOTE: It is easy to have roasted garlic on hand. See SMART GRILLING on page 109, or prepare according to the note accompanying TOMATO, BANANA PEPPER, AND POLE BEAN SALSA on page 164.

THE TRUTH ABOUT KNIVES

Your knife collection does not have to be extensive and the knives don't have to match, but they should be top quality so that, when the blades are sharpened, they hold their edge. Sharp knives are far safer than dull ones, which is important when you are chopping a lot of vegetables. Also, sharp knives don't bruise vegetables or fruits, so they won't bleed or spoil.

You should be outfitted with a 10- or 12-inch chef's knife, an 8-inch chef's knife, a paring knife, a boning knife, and a serrated knife. The blades should extend all the way to the end of the handle and be secured with three rivets. High-carbon stainless steel is the most practical material for most people. It won't stain or rust and holds its edge longer than other materials, although it needs a harder sharpening steel than carbon steel or stainless steel. Sharpen your knifes every time you use them. That way, they will always be sharp and reaching for the sharpener is a good habit to develop.

You will have to decide how best to sharpen your knives. I use a whetstone, but you may prefer a sharpening steel, an electric sharpener, or an abrasive wheel. Be sure to buy a highly rated electric sharpener, as low-quality ones can damage knives.

Keep your knives clean, dry, and sharp. Wash them by hand with warm, soapy water and dry them with a towel. The blades can dull and nick if they knock around in the dishwasher. Ditto for storing: Keep them in a knife block or on a rack, rather than in a drawer.

PISTACHIO PORK LOIN CHOPS
with Pumpkin Sauce

**SERVES
6**

JUST AS PICKING THE RIGHT TOMATO MAKES THE DIFFERENCE between a mediocre tomato salad and a truly memorable one, choosing the right pork promises an outstanding dish. Much of the pork sold in supermarkets is mass-produced from animals rushed to maturity at the expense of flavor, texture, and, sadly, the environment. Instead, look for naturally raised pork, preferably from a local farm.

Pork is sweet, which is why when we cook it in the fall, we are drawn to the wonderful sweet-ness of tree fruits, such as apples or pears. As delicious as these are, I also like to cook pork with pumpkins or winter squashes, which provide an entirely different, but equally pleasing, under-lying sweetness when roasted.

Pumpkins and nuts are natural partners, of course, but you may not immediately think of pistachios for a pork recipe. Unlike other nuts,

they have an aromatic quality that adds great character to nearly any food with which they are paired.

I also temper the spices, a fantastic technique I picked up in India and one that has stayed with me more than anything else I learned there. Indian chefs temper spices in ghee, but I use a flavorless oil for this process. The tempered spices are combined with the squash and then other ingredients and puréed until the flavors come together in a slightly textured sauce.

FLAVORLESS VEGETABLE OIL SPRAY or rice or grapeseed oil in a mister or spray bottle

4 POUNDS PUMPKIN, butternut squash, or Hokkaido squash, peeled, seeded, and cut into 1-inch cubes (about 16 cups)

SALT AND FRESHLY GROUND BLACK PEPPER

2 TABLESPOONS RICE OR GRAPE-SEED OIL, plus more for misting if needed

1 TEASPOON BLACK MUSTARD SEEDS

½ CUP DICED YELLOW ONION

1 LARGE CLOVE GARLIC, thinly sliced

1 TABLESPOON CORIANDER SEEDS

2 GREEN CARDAMOM PODS

1 LONG CINNAMON STICK

3 TO 4 TABLESPOONS WATER

12 FRESH LEMON VERBENA LEAVES, thinly sliced

¼ CUP SLICED FRESH CHERVIL LEAVES AND STEMS

4 OUNCES SHELLED PISTACHIOS, GROUND (about 1 cup ground)

¼ CUP ROUGHLY CHOPPED FRESH MARJORAM LEAVES

SIX 6-OUNCE BONELESS PORK LOIN CHOPS, each about 1 inch thick

1. Preheat the oven to 400°F.

2. Spray about two-thirds of the squash cubes with vegetable oil spray and then season with salt and pepper. Set aside the remaining cubes.

3. Spread the seasoned cubes on a large rimmed baking sheet or pan so that the cubes are not touching and bake, turning once, for 20 to 30 minutes, or until the cubes soften and begin to brown.

4. Meanwhile, juice the remaining squash cubes in a heavy-duty juicer. You will have about ⅔ cup juice. (Discard the pulp, or freeze for use in muffins or breakfast breads.)

5. Heat a large saucepan over medium heat until hot. Add the 2 tablespoons oil and the mustard seeds and sauté for 20 to 30 seconds, or until the seeds begin to pop. Add the onion and sauté for about 2 minutes, or until the onion begins to brown. Add the garlic, coriander seeds, cardamom pods, and cinnamon stick and sauté for about 1 minute, or until the garlic browns lightly.

6. Add the squash juice and roasted squash cubes. Reduce the heat to medium-low and simmer, stirring constantly, for 8 to 10 minutes, or until the juices begin to thicken. Stir in enough of the water to blend and thin a little. Remove the cinnamon stick and discard. Working in batches, transfer the sauce to a blender and process until smooth. You will have about 2½ cups purée.

7. Return the purée to the saucepan, stir in the lemon verbena and chervil, and cover to keep warm.

8. Heat 2 large cast-iron skillets, each one large enough to hold the pork chops in a single layer, over medium-high heat, or preheat a countertop grill, such as a George Foreman grill.

9. In a small bowl, toss the ground pistachios and marjoram. Season each pork chop on both sides with salt and pepper and then firmly press the pistachio-herb mixture into both sides of each chop. If you are using the two-skillet method, mist each pork chop lightly with rice or grapeseed oil.

10. When the skillets are hot, put the pork chops in 1 skillet and immediately set the second skillet on top, so that the bottom of the top skillet presses on the chops. Turn the heat to low and let the chops cook in the hot pans for 6 to 8 minutes, or until an instant-read thermometer registers 145°F. If you are using the countertop grill, grill the pork chops for about 8 minutes, or until cooked through and an instant-read thermometer registers 145°F.

11. Transfer the chops to plates. Reheat the purée gently until hot, pour into a serving bowl, and pass at the table.

SKILLET PORK ROAST
with Garden Vegetable and Eggplant Sauce

**SERVES
6**

**WHILE THIS IS NOTHING MORE COMPLICATED THAN
A MEAL IN A SKILLET**, the trick is finding a skillet
large enough to hold a three-pound pork loin
plus the garden vegetables. Once you locate it,
the rest is easy. It's cool how with just the liquid
from the tomatoes and eggplant, you end up
with such a beautiful sauce. You may feel you
are overcooking the green beans, but don't be
alarmed. They may be softer than you are used
to, but they add to the overall flavor of the sauce,
bolstered most significantly by the sweet flavor
from the roasted vegetables. You can remove
the beans from the pan earlier than specified if
you want, but I say go all the way! Use a wooden
spoon to scrape up all the browned bits from
the pork when deglazing the pan. These add
immeasurably to the final flavor of the sauce,
too.

ONE 3-POUND BONELESS PORK LOIN ROAST, preferably cut from the shoulder end

SALT AND FRESHLY GROUND BLACK PEPPER

2 TABLESPOONS OLIVE OIL

2 EGGPLANTS (about 1½ pounds total), cut lengthwise into ½-inch-thick slices

3 LARGE FRESH THYME SPRIGS

3 LARGE FRESH SAGE SPRIGS

6 CARROTS, peeled and halved lengthwise

8 OUNCES GREEN BEANS, stems trimmed and any strings removed

2 LARGE VINE-RIPENED TOMATOES (about 1¼ pounds total)

¼ CUP EXTRA-VIRGIN OLIVE OIL

1. Preheat the oven to 375°F. Select a cast-iron skillet large enough to hold the pork loin with plenty of room to spare and place over medium-high heat.

2. Season the pork roast with salt and pepper. When the skillet is hot, add the oil, then sear the roast for about 5 minutes, turning once or twice so that it's nicely browned on all sides. Scoot the roast over to the side of the skillet and add as much eggplant in a single layer as needed to fill the empty space in the pan. You may have to cut the eggplant slices into wedges to make them fit. Rest 1 thyme sprig and 1 sage sprig on the pork roast. Transfer the pan to the oven and roast for about 10 minutes, or until the eggplant browns lightly on the bottom. Turn the eggplant over and roast for 10 minutes longer, or until browned and soft.

3. Remove the cooked eggplant and then add the remaining eggplant to the pan and cook it in the same way. Set aside all the eggplant to cool.

4. Add the carrots to the pan and roast the pork for about 10 minutes longer, or until an instant-read thermometer registers 140°F. At this point, add the green beans to the skillet and cook for 15 to 20 minutes, or until the pork reaches an internal temperature of 150°F.

5. Meanwhile, chop the cooled eggplant into small dice. Core and halve the tomatoes, then chop the halves into pieces about the same size as the eggplant.

6. Transfer the pork, carrots, and beans to a warmed platter and tent with aluminum foil to keep warm. Discard the cooked thyme and sage branches. Skim and discard as much fat as possible from the pan juices.

7. Add the eggplant, tomatoes, and remaining 2 sprigs each thyme and sage to the skillet over medium-high heat and bring to a simmer. Cook uncovered, stirring frequently with a wooden spoon and pressing on the vegetables to blend them into a thick and chunky sauce, for 12 to 15 minutes, or until the vegetables break down and develop a saucelike consistency. Add the olive oil, reduce the heat to low, and cook for 2 to 3 minutes, or until the sauce emulsifies. Season to taste with salt and pepper.

8. Slice the pork roast and serve the pork, carrots, and beans with the sauce spooned over them.

BAKED FRESH HAM

with Roasted Apple and Almond Salad

**SERVES
6 TO 8**

ROASTED FRESH HAM IS JUST AS TASTY AS PORK LOIN BUT IS FAR LESS EXPENSIVE, and I highly recommend that pork lovers try it. I also find it to be moister and more tender. Fresh ham takes longer to cook than pork loin, but this just means your house smells good even longer. It is not smoked and is not pink, and should not be thought of for sandwiches alone—though it makes delicious ones. Fresh ham tastes like pork loin, so it's not surprising that it pairs well with many of the same ingredients, such as apples and onions.

In the fall, when you harvest onions and crisp apples, roast them alongside the ham in this wonderful recipe. They will caramelize and pack a powerful wallop. Of course, applesauce is always a good bet with pork, so if you would like to serve it, too, see the recipe on page 166. I can't tell you how good this baked ham is. You'll spend less and gain more when it comes to flavor.

continued

baked fresh ham
with roasted apple and almond salad

continued

2 CUPS (about 10 ounces) **BLANCHED WHOLE ALMONDS**

¼ CUP CORIANDER SEEDS

ONE 7- TO 8-POUND RUMP-END FRESH HAM, trimmed and tied

SALT AND FRESHLY GROUND BLACK PEPPER

2 CUPS FRESHLY PRESSED APPLE JUICE or apple cider

2 CINNAMON STICKS

6 GREEN CARDAMOM PODS

1 SWEET ONION such as Vidalia or Walla Walla, cut into ½-inch-thick slices

2 POUNDS FIRM, CRISP BAKING APPLES such as locally grown Granny Smith, Roxbury Russet, pippin, or Empire, cored and cut into 1-inch chunks

1 CUP LOOSELY PACKED FRESH CILANTRO LEAVES

1. Preheat the oven to 350°F.

2. Spread the almonds on a baking sheet and toast, stirring once or twice, for 6 to 8 minutes, or until lightly browned. Set aside.

3. In a small, dry skillet, toast the coriander seeds, shaking the pan often, for about 1½ minutes, or until the seeds smell like oranges. Immediately pour into a small dish and let cool. When cool, grind in a spice grinder or coffee grinder reserved for spices to the consistency of coarse meal. Set aside.

4. Rub the ham with salt and pepper and put it in a roasting pan large enough to hold it with enough space for the onion slices and apples. Add the apple juice, cinnamon, and cardamom to the pan and roast for 2 to 2½ hours, or until an instant-read thermometer inserted near the center of the roast, but not touching the bone, registers 140°F.

5. Remove the pan from the oven and, without removing the ham from the pan, skim as much fat as possible from the juices. Add the onion slices and apples to the pan, return the pan to the oven, and increase the oven temperature to 400°F. Roast for about 20 minutes longer, or until the ham reaches an internal temperature of 150°F and the onion and apples begin to brown. The ham should bake for 20 to 25 minutes per pound. Do not overcook.

6. Transfer the ham to a cutting board or platter, cover with a clean kitchen towel or tent with aluminum foil to hold in moisture, and let rest for 15 minutes.

7. Transfer the onion and apples to a large bowl. Scrape the bottom and sides of the roasting pan with a wooden spoon to dislodge all the browned bits and juices and add to the bowl. Toss in the toasted almonds and ground coriander and season lightly with salt and pepper. Add the cilantro and toss gently to distribute evenly.

8. Slice the ham and serve with the apple and almond salad.

Two-Skillet
HERB-ROASTED CHICKEN
with Yukon Gold Home Fries

**SERVES
6**

I RECALL A BUSY NIGHT WHEN I WAS WORKING IN A RESTAURANT AND REALIZED I was about fifteen minutes behind on a roasted chicken for a table of six. After I wasted a few minutes panicking, I butterfly-boned a whole baby chicken, grabbed two sauté pans, heated them over the fire, and then pressed the chicken between the hot pans before roasting it in the hottest oven on the line. The result was amazing! To my surprise, the herbs slipped under the skin smelled more aromatic than usual, the skin was extremely crisp, and the chicken cooked in plenty of time to make it to the table with the rest of the entrées. Best of all, the customer said it was one of the best chickens she had ever eaten. A happy accident turned into a new cooking method.

I use cast-iron skillets in my home kitchen, which are heavy enough to weight the chicken effortlessly and which most home cooks have on hand. If you don't, they are not hard to find. Turn to page 59 for more on the care of these stupendous cooking tools. Most butchers will gladly butterfly-bone a small bird for you if you give them enough notice. Ask the butcher to remove the thigh bones. And it's not hard to do yourself if you want to get to know your chicken better!

continued

two-skillet herb-roasted chicken
with yukon gold home fries

continued

8 FRESH THYME SPRIGS

**TWO 2½– TO 3-POUND CHICKENS,
BUTTERFLY-BONED**
(see Note)

4 YUKON GOLD POTATOES,
cut into ½-inch-thick slices

**SALT AND FRESHLY GROUND
BLACK PEPPER**

GRAPESEED OR RICE OIL
in a mister or spray bottle

8 FRESH SAGE SPRIGS

1. Select 4 large cast-iron skillets, each one large enough to hold 1 chicken in comfortably. Put 2 skillets in the oven and preheat the oven to 425°F.

2. Starting from the body cavity, and being careful not to tear the skin, slip your fingers between the skin and flesh of 1 chicken to create a pocket on each breast and each leg-thigh portion. Slip a thyme sprig into each pocket, spreading the herb as evenly as possible over the meat. Repeat with the second chicken and the remaining thyme.

3. Heat the other 2 cast-iron skillets on the stove top over medium-high heat. Meanwhile, season the potato slices with salt and pepper and mist lightly with oil.

4. Put 1 chicken, skin side down, in one of the hot skillets on the stove top. Position the bird so that the leg-thigh portions are closest to the handle of each pan. Arrange half the potato slices around the chicken on the exposed surface of the pan. Put the other chicken and the remaining potatoes in the other hot skillet.

5. Cook for about 4 minutes, or until the skin of both chickens is lightly browned. Turn the chickens over, but make sure the leg-thigh portions are still closest to the handle. Turn the potatoes over. Set a a sage sprig over each breast and each leg-thigh portion.

6. Using a thick oven mitt, remove the hot skillets from the oven and put one on top of each chicken so that they press down on the meat and the handles of the skillets are aligned. Return to the oven and roast for about 30 minutes. Remove the top skillets, making sure the sage stays in place. Turn the potatoes again and return the skillets holding the chickens and potatoes to the oven for about 10 minutes longer, or until the chickens are cooked through. The chickens should be crispy on the outside and moist on the inside and the potatoes will have taken on the flavor of the herbs and chicken.

7. Serve the chickens with the potatoes alongside.

NOTE: To butterfly-bone a chicken, split it down the back and remove the backbone and rib cage. This is most commonly done when a cook wants to broil a whole chicken with the skin on.

OREGANO CHICKEN
with Grilled Kale and Heirloom Tomatoes

SERVES
6

THIS RECIPE CELEBRATES KALE. The heirloom tomatoes deserve equal time, but they're easy to tout: Everyone loves them. Kale gets a bum rap, even from chef friends of mine who complain about how tired they get of "braising greens" as fall and winter go on. My mom would take them out to the woodshed for that kind of talk! I find kale brilliant when braised and awesome when grilled. The season for kale runs from midsummer far into the fall, and if you have it in the garden, you will want to use it often. I grow both green and purple kale and love to experiment with other cultivars such as Russian Red, Tuscan kale, and curly kale.

Admittedly, this is a summer recipe, but you can grill kale all year long—meat isn't the only thing that tastes good with a little charring! For this recipe, I serve the kale with grilled chicken and raw tomatoes, but it would taste equally good with grilled apples or squash or as a bed for roasted fish. In the wintertime, brush grilled winter kale with summer preserves and serve it with pork roast. Sensational!

continued

6 BONELESS, SKINLESS CHICKEN BREAST HALVES

¼ **CUP EXTRA-VIRGIN OLIVE OIL**

½ **CUP BALSAMIC VINEGAR**

1 CUP COARSELY CHOPPED FRESH OREGANO or summer savory leaves

4 SCALLIONS, white and green parts, thinly sliced

2 TEASPOONS FRESHLY CRACKED BLACK PEPPER

SALT

1 TABLESPOON GRAPESEED OIL

6 LARGE GREEN KALE LEAVES

6 LARGE PURPLE KALE LEAVES

6 HEIRLOOM TOMATOES (try for different colors and varieties such as Cherokee Purple, Brandywine, Daddy Sunshine, and Green Zebra)

FRESHLY GROUND BLACK PEPPER

1 CUP ASSORTED FRESH BASIL LEAVES AND TOPS (where the herb bolts) such as purple, Thai, and/or lemon

1. Put the chicken breasts in a shallow nonreactive dish.

2. In a small bowl, whisk together the olive oil, vinegar, oregano, scallions, and cracked pepper. Pour this mixture over the chicken, turn the chicken breasts to coat, cover, and refrigerate for 2 hours to marinate.

3. Prepare a charcoal or gas grill for grilling over a medium-hot fire. If using charcoal, mound the coals to one side of the grill for indirect grilling. If using a gas grill, turn one of the burners to low. Lightly oil the grill grate.

4. Lift the chicken from the marinade and let as much marinade as possible drip back into the bowl, scraping it off as necessary. Set the marinade aside. Season the chicken breasts on both sides with salt. Place the chicken over the hottest part of the grill and cook, turning once, until the chicken is well marked on both sides. This should take 5 to 6 minutes. Move the chicken breasts to the cooler section of the grill and grill indirectly for about 3 minutes on each side, or until cooked through and an instant-read thermometer registers 155°F. Transfer the chicken breasts to a warmed platter and cover to keep warm.

5. Pour the reserved marinade into a small saucepan, place on the hottest part of the grill, bring to a boil, and simmer for 5 minutes. (You can instead do this over a burner on your stove.)

6. Brush both sides of the kale leaves with the grapeseed oil and season lightly with salt. Grill the leaves for 1 to 2 minutes, or until they are brown and smell smoky. If parts of the leaves appear slightly burned, you have achieved succulence—trust me.

7. Core and slice the tomatoes, then arrange them with the kale leaves, slightly overlapping them shingle fashion, next to the chicken on the platter. Drizzle the platter with the hot marinade and season with salt and ground pepper. Liberally sprinkle the platter with the basil. Serve at once.

ROAST CHICKEN
with Pear, Apple, and Goat Cheese Gratin

SERVES
4 TO 6

ALTHOUGH THEY MAY BE HARD TO FIND, POUSSINS, YOUNG, SMALL, TENDER CHICKENS, are well worth the search. If you must, however, you can substitute Cornish game hens for them. Interestingly, there are a variety of producers at farmers' markets who might grow birds to the size you wish, as long as you purchase the bird in advance. It's worth the wait, especially when anticipation makes the heart grow fonder.

Here, I pair the poussins with a gratin of fall tree fruits. The best come straight from the orchard, so look for growers in your area. Or, load the kids in the car for a "pick-your-own" excursion. So many Saturdays or Sundays are spent with parents reading the paper and kids either watching cartoons or playing video games. Picking apples is a great way for the entire family to spend a few hours together while guaranteeing better tasting and healthier meals.

Pack a light lunch (Riesling wine for the grown-ups), head for an apple orchard, and grab some of the best apples you'll ever eat! Apples are commercially grown in thirty-six states, so there is a good chance you'll be able to find a place where you can pick your own. If not, look for regionally grown apples at your local farmers' market.

For this recipe, the goat and Cheddar cheeses combine to make a gratin rich and meltingly delicious for an overall terrific fall dish. These flavors pair amazingly well with the tart-sweet apples and pears. Wimpy, insipid storage apples from the other side of the country or halfway around the globe need not apply!

4 POUSSINS OR CORNISH GAME HENS, 1¼ to 1½ pounds (the smaller the better), trimmed of fat

2 TABLESPOONS GRAPESEED OR RICE OIL

16 SMALL FRESH THYME SPRIGS

FINE SEA SALT AND FRESHLY GROUND BLACK PEPPER

3 LARGE, TART APPLES such as Granny Smith, Jonagold, or Cortland, peeled and cored

2 SLIGHTLY UNDERRIPE GOOD-SIZED PEARS such as Bosc or Anjou, peeled and cored

1 SMALL SWEET ONION such as Vidalia or Walla Walla, very thinly sliced

⅓ CUP CRUMBLED FRESH GOAT CHEESE (about 2 ounces)

1 TABLESPOON FRESH THYME LEAVES

2 TABLESPOONS FRESH BREAD CRUMBS

2 TABLESPOONS FRESHLY GRATED CHEDDAR CHEESE (about ½ ounce)

2 CUPS FRESHLY PRESSED APPLE JUICE or apple cider

1. Preheat the oven to 375°F. Position a rack in the bottom third of the oven. Rinse the poussins inside and out and pat dry. Coat a roasting pan just large enough to hold the birds comfortably with grapeseed oil.

2. Carefully loosen the skin from the chicken breasts by working your fingers between the skin and the meat without making any tears. Insert a thyme sprig between the skin and meat of each breast. Where the tail bones join the cavities, make more pockets between the skin and meat of each thigh. Insert a thyme sprig in each. Rub the top of each bird with about 1 teaspoon oil to help them brown and season generously inside and out with salt and pepper. Tuck the wings under the back and tie the legs together.

3. Put the chickens, breast side down, in the roasting pan. Roast for 15 minutes. Turn the chickens over (breast side up) and roast for 20 minutes longer. Increase the heat to 425°F and roast for 10 to 12 minutes, or until the skin is nicely browned and the juices run clear when thickest part of a thigh is pierced with a small knife.

4. While the chickens are roasting, use a French or Japanese mandoline to slice the apples and pears very thin. On a nonstick 11-by-17-inch baking sheet, arrange half of the apple slices, shingle fashion, in a circle large enough in circumference to hold the birds. Spread one-third of the onion evenly over the apple slices and then sprinkle with one-third of the crumbled goat cheese and one-third of the thyme leaves. Arrange all the pear slices, shingle fashion, over the top and sprinkle with one-half of the remaining onion, goat cheese, and thyme leaves. Top with the remaining apple slices, followed by the remaining onion, goat cheese, and thyme leaves. In a small bowl, combine the bread crumbs and the Cheddar cheese. Sprinkle the mixture over the final goat cheese layer.

5. Place the gratin in the oven with the chicken (or use another oven) for about 15 minutes, or until the crust is browned and the Cheddar cheese is thoroughly melted. Remove the gratin and cover loosely with foil to keep warm.

6. When the chickens are ready, remove them from the oven, tent loosely with aluminum foil, and let rest for 12 minutes before serving. Do not turn off the oven. Defat the pan juices and set the roasting pan on the stove top over high heat. Add the apple juice and bring to a boil. Cook, scraping up the browned bits from the bottom and sides of the pan and stirring constantly, for 5 to 6 minutes, or until the liquid is reduced by half. Pour the sauce into a gravy boat or pitcher and keep warm.

7. Return the gratin to the oven for less than a minute, just to heat up. Carefully slide it onto the center of a warmed serving platter and arrange the birds on top in pinwheel fashion. Drizzle the platter with a little of the sauce and pass the remainder at the table.

GRILLED EGGPLANT PARMESAN

**SERVES
6**

JUST AS SO MANY GARDENERS HAVE JOYFULLY DISCOVERED HEIRLOOM TOMATOES, some are now taking the same journey with eggplants. Despite popular conceptions, the norm for eggplant is no more dark purple than the norm for grapes is green or for apples red. Eggplants can be white, green, red, orange, rose, deep or light purple, striped, or variegated. They can be small, round, long, slender, plump, or pear shaped. While it's nearly impossible to generalize, those from Asia often tend to be long and slender and white or light colored and those from Europe larger and darker—although white eggplants are grown in Italy and deep purple eggplants are popular in Japan. Green eggplants may originally have been grown in Southeast Asia, but some strains were developed in the United States.

While some eggplants are more tender, some have thinner skins, and some cook more quickly, none holds its shape during cooking and all have mild flavor. They are integral to vegetarian cooking, and so it's not hard to find ways to cook them. Eggplants are easy to start from seed and easy to grow in the garden. Once you start investigating the different varieties, I bet you'll be as hooked as I am. Few garden vegetables are as beautiful to behold or as delicious to eat.

Here, I take a decidedly healthful look at a classic, eggplant Parmesan. I like to use Italian white or purple eggplants because of their sturdy skin and high-moisture flesh. The tomatoes must be perfectly ripe. If you can't find good tomatoes, use a top-grade canned product such as Muir Glen. Because I cook for well-being, in this recipe I forgo the customary egg wash and breading and instead split the eggplant and grill it.

1 LARGE OR 2 SMALL RIPE TOMATOES (about 1 pound total), cored and cut into ¼-inch-thick slices

2 TABLESPOONS EXTRA-VIRGIN OLIVE OIL

3 FRESH BAY LEAVES or ¾ cup thinly sliced fresh basil leaves

SALT AND FRESHLY GROUND BLACK PEPPER

3 WHITE OR SMALL, SLENDER PURPLE EGGPLANTS (2 to 2½ pounds total), halved lengthwise

2 TABLESPOONS GRAPESEED OIL

½ CUP GRATED PARMESAN CHEESE

1. Put the tomato slices in a saucepan and sprinkle with the olive oil. Set over medium heat and cook, stirring gently only to prevent sticking, for 2 to 3 minutes, or until the tomatoes begin to soften. Add the bay or basil leaves, remove the pan from the heat, and set aside for 30 minutes.

2. If you used bay leaves, remove them and transfer the tomatoes to a blender or food processor. Purée until smooth; you should have about 2 cups. Season to taste with salt and pepper and set aside.

3. Prepare a charcoal or gas grill for grilling over a medium-hot fire. Lightly oil the grill grate.

4. Coat the eggplant halves with the grapeseed oil and season well with salt and pepper. Place the eggplants, skin side down, over the hottest part of the fire and grill for 15 to 20 minutes, or until the skin blackens, the juice boils up through the flesh, and the flesh is tender but not mushy. The timing will depend on the thickness of the eggplant. Use tongs to move the eggplants during grilling so that they cook evenly.

5. Make an indentation about 1 inch deep in the flesh of each eggplant half and spoon a generous amount of the puréed tomatoes into each indentation. Don't hold back! Grill for about 5 minutes longer, or until the sauce is hot. For a slightly smoky flavor, cover the grill. Sprinkle evenly with the Parmesan cheese and grill for a few minutes, or just until the cheese begins to melt. If you have more sauce, use a fork to push down the soft flesh of the eggplant and spoon more sauce into the indentation. Serve immediately.

SMART GRILLING

When you fire up the charcoal or gas grill, plan ahead. If, for instance, you have bell peppers, eggplant, or garlic in the kitchen, grill them alongside whatever else you are cooking. You can store the grilled peppers covered with oil, which keeps them longer, or simply slip them into plastic bags. Grilled eggplant will keep for a few days in rigid plastic containers or plastic bags. Grilled garlic, like roasted garlic (see the note accompanying TOMATO, BANANA PEPPER, AND POLE BEAN SALSA on page 164), is soft and pulpy. Wrap the head or collection of cloves in plastic or put them in a plastic bag, refrigerate, and squeeze the pulp from the individual cloves as needed.

You can employ this smart grilling for all sorts of vegetables and fruits: potatoes, squashes, tomatoes, mushrooms, onions, apples—you name it. All of them are tasty in salads or sandwiches, and you'll be glad you thought about grilling them ahead of time.

EGGPLANT, GOAT CHEESE, and TOMATO
Casserole

SERVES
8 TO 10

I GROW A LOT OF EGGPLANTS IN THE GARDEN mainly because they are such an outstanding ingredient in so many dishes, but also because they look great. I like to grow different types in varying sizes and colors, and am on an unabashed mission to entice others to experiment with the many varieties available from Seeds of Change (see Sources, page 221) and other heirloom-seed companies. All eggplants are sufficiently hearty and therefore withstand most soil types and climates.

When eggplant cooks, it shrinks and releases a lot of moisture, which explains why many cooks feel eggplant dishes are too wet. I avoid this by precooking the vegetable. Over the years, home cooks have gotten the idea that they must salt and press eggplant before cooking it to rid it of excess moisture and bitterness, but I say "hogwash!" to this, particularly if you

use fresh eggplants from your garden or a farm stand. In this recipe, I eliminate the excess juices by pre-cooking the eggplant slices. This dries the slices while concentrating their flavor. Look for heavy, firm eggplants with vibrant color. The stem end should be green and fresh looking; the opposite end will be a little green on a dark eggplant and blemish free on a white eggplant. I promise, if you use garden-fresh eggplants, they never will be bitter.

When I make this casserole, I assemble everything while it's still warm, which means the finished dish takes very little time to heat through. Without question, it takes some time to make, but if you do it right, the flavors are so pure and focused that you won't need to add extra seasoning or spices.

6 VINE-RIPENED HEIRLOOM
TOMATOES (about 3 pounds total)

SALT AND FRESHLY GROUND
BLACK PEPPER

2 YELLOW ONIONS, thinly sliced

7 TABLESPOONS GRAPESEED
OR RICE OIL

I FENNEL BULB, trimmed and
thinly sliced lengthwise

2 TABLESPOONS WATER

3 LARGE, DARK PURPLE
EGGPLANTS such as Black Beauty
(about 3 1/2 pounds total)

2 OR 3 SLENDER LAVENDER
ASIAN EGGPLANTS
(about 2 pounds total)

6 GENEROUS FRESH BASIL
SPRIGS

10 OUNCES FRESH GOAT CHEESE

I TABLESPOON FRESH
THYME LEAVES

1/4 CUP FRESHLY GRATED
ROMANO CHEESE

1. Preheat the oven to 200°F.

2. Core the tomatoes and cut in half through the equator. Hold the tomato halves over a glass bowl and gently squeeze to remove some of the seeds and juice. Reserve the seeds and juice. Carefully cut each tomato half into thick slices, season with salt and pepper, and put on a rimmed baking sheet.

3. Roast the tomato slices for 2 hours, or until they are slightly dried but still moist. Set aside at room temperature until needed. Increase the oven temperature to 350°F.

4. Toss the onions with 2 tablespoons of the oil. Heat a nonstick sauté pan over medium-high heat. When hot, add the onions and cook for 2 to 3 minutes, or until they begin to brown. Reduce the heat to medium and cook, stirring occasionally, for 4 to 5 minutes, or until golden and caramelized. Remove the onions from the pan and set aside. You will have about 1 cup.

5. Add 1 tablespoon oil to the pan, and then add the fennel. (It is likely the pan will be brown from caramelizing the onions. The dark brown film will add great caramelized onion flavor to the fennel.) Set over medium heat, cover, and, after about 3 minutes, the fennel will begin to cook (you will hear it sizzle). Lift the lid and add the water. Re-cover and cook, occasionally lifting the lid to stir with a flat wooden or metal spatula while the moisture from the fennel naturally deglazes the browned bits from the pan, for 5 to 7 minutes longer, or until the fennel is tender. Set aside.

continued

6. If desired, peel the purple eggplants (depending on the freshness of the eggplant and your preference). Cut all the eggplants lengthwise into ½-inch-thick slices. Brush or mist both sides of each slice with the remaining 4 tablespoons oil and season with salt and pepper.

7. Lay 2 of the basil sprigs in a preheated ridged grill pan on the stove top or on the surface of a countertop grill, such as a George Foreman grill. Lay some eggplant slices on top of the basil. Cover the pan or close the lid of the grill. Cook over medium heat, turning once, for 15 minutes, or until the eggplant is well browned. The eggplant is ready when steam stops escaping from the pan or the grill. Remove the eggplant and basil to a platter or tray in a single layer and repeat with the remaining basil and eggplant in 2 more batches. As you remove the eggplant, keep the large and slender eggplant slices separate.

8. Meanwhile, in a food processor, combine the goat cheese, thyme, and the reserved tomato juice and seeds and pulse several times until a spreadable mixture forms. Season to taste with salt and pepper.

9. Lay the eggplant with the basil on it on a work surface and spread each slice with 1 to 2 tablespoons of the goat cheese mixture.

10. Arrange half of the reserved oven-dried tomatoes on the bottom of a deep 9-inch square baking dish. Top with a layer of the large eggplant slices followed by a layer of all the smaller eggplant slices, both cheese side up. Distribute the sautéed fennel over the top and then follow with another layer of large eggplant slices, cheese side up. Evenly distribute the caramelized onions over the top and then the remaining large eggplant slices. Evenly distribute the remaining roasted tomatoes over the top and sprinkle with the Romano cheese.

11. Bake uncovered for 25 to 30 minutes, or until the casserole is bubbling and heated through and the grated cheese melts. Serve immediately.

Kabocha Squash RISOTTO

SERVES 6

NOT SURPRISINGLY, A CHALLENGE I FACED WHEN I BEGAN COOKING FOR WELL-BEING WAS MAKING RISOTTO WITHOUT BUTTER OR CHEESE. How could I re-create that seductive smoothness that makes risotto such a favorite? I began by using squash juice because I knew the natural starch would help the juice thicken while cooking. Unfortunately, I found it was too sticky, leaving the risotto with a consistency similar to that of okra. On a hunch, I made the risotto with vegetable stock and then finished it with squash juice, which worked very much like cheese and butter does in traditional risotto: The stickiness disappeared and the rice took on a creaminess made better by the boost of squash flavor. Nature was on my side.

continued

ONE 1½- TO 2-POUND KABOCHA
SQUASH

SALT AND FRESHLY GROUND
BLACK PEPPER

I LARGE SWEET ONION such as
Vidalia or Walla Walla, cut into ½-inch-thick
slices

½ CUP EXTRA-VIRGIN OLIVE OIL

2 TABLESPOONS DICED SHALLOT

2 CINNAMON STICKS

2 CUPS CARNAROLI, ARBORIO,
OR VIALONE NANO RICE

6½ CUPS SIMPLE VEGETABLE
STOCK (page 57)

I FRESH BAY LEAF OR BASIL LEAF

1½ CUPS KABOCHA SQUASH JUICE
(see JUICING FRUITS AND
VEGETABLES, page 180)

1½ CUPS COARSELY CHOPPED
ROASTED, PEELED CHESTNUTS
(about 30 chestnuts) (see Note)

3 TABLESPOONS MINCED
FRESH CHIVES

I. Preheat the oven to 300°F.

2. Halve the squash and remove the seeds and strings. Rinse the seeds and spread them on a dry kitchen towel or other surface to dry. Peel the squash and cut into ½-inch cubes. Measure 3 cups. (Use any extra squash in another dish.)

3. Spread the squash seeds on a rimmed baking sheet, sprinkle with salt and pepper, and roast for about 35 minutes, or until crisp and lightly browned. Stir them several times during cooking so they brown evenly. Transfer to a plate to cool. Set aside.

4. Increase the oven temperature to 400°F.

5. Brush the onion slices on both sides with 2 tablespoons of the oil and season with salt and pepper. Spread on a baking sheet and roast, turning once, for 15 to 20 minutes, or until lightly browned. Let cool and then cut into ½-inch cubes.

6. Heat 4 tablespoons of the oil in a very large saucepan over medium heat. Add the shallot and cinnamon sticks and sauté for about 5 minutes, or until the shallot is translucent. Add the rice and cook, stirring constantly, for 2 to 3 minutes, or until the kernels are opaque. Do not let the rice brown.

7. Add about 2 cups of the stock. Cook, stirring constantly, until the stock is absorbed by the rice. Add 1 more cup of the stock and cook, stirring, until the stock is absorbed. Add another cup of stock and the bay leaf or basil leaf and cook, stirring and adding stock 1 cup at a time as each addition is absorbed, until all but ½ cup of the stock is absorbed. Reserve the ½ cup stock. The entire process will take 20 to 25 minutes.

8. Remove the cinnamon sticks and the bay leaf, if used. Spread the risotto on a rimmed baking sheet and cover with parchment paper. Let cool to room temperature.

9. Heat the remaining 2 tablespoons oil in the same large saucepan, add the squash cubes, and cook over medium heat for about 8 minutes, or until the squash begins to soften. Add the roasted onion and cook for about 5 minutes longer, or until the squash is cooked through. Add the reserved ½ cup stock and the cooled risotto.

continued

kabocha squash risotto

continued

10. Cook, stirring constantly but gently, for about 3 minutes, or until the rice heats and absorbs the stock. Add the squash juice and cook, stirring, for 3 to 4 minutes, or until the risotto is creamy. Season to taste with salt and pepper.

11. Spoon the risotto into warmed bowls. Garnish with the chestnuts, chives, and roasted squash seeds.

NOTE: To roast chestnuts, score an X in the flat side of each nut with a sharp knife without cutting through the nut meat. Spread the nuts in a single layer in a shallow ungreased baking pan and roast in a 350°F oven for about 15 minutes, or until the nuts are fragrant and the scored portions of the shells begin to separate from the nut meat. Transfer to a plate and, when cool enough to handle but still warm, use your fingers or a knife to peel off the outer shell and inner skin.

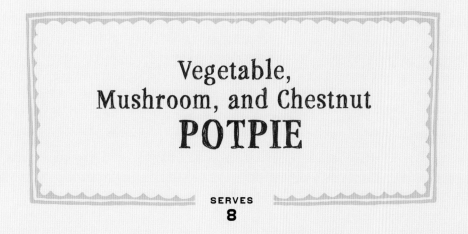

Vegetable, Mushroom, and Chestnut POTPIE

SERVES 8

WHEN I WROTE *TASTE: PURE AND SIMPLE,* I HAD THE NAGGING FEELING THAT I had failed my readers by not including recipes that dealt creatively with leftovers. They can be used in wonderful ways, such as this potpie.

Throwing food away is depressing, wasteful, and can cause a home cook to feel he or she has squandered time and money. This was never true of my mom. She looked at leftovers the way a squirrel looks at an acorn-laden oak tree, a raccoon looks at a chicken coop, and the woodchuck eyes my collards! The point is, my mom had tremendous success using leftovers. From her I learned that the better you deal with them, the better you feel about cooking at home.

Vegetables are a common leftover and too often find their way to a forgotten corner of the refrigerator. When I have a backlog of vegetables in the refrigerator, I treat the family to this potpie. It's best if I have pumpkin soup on hand. If not, any creamy-style soup leftovers will do. During baking, the leftover soup in the pie is absorbed by the vegetables, which take on a pleasant but discernable dry mouthfeel. This is why I like to serve the pie with extra-virgin olive oil for drizzling, and for the grown-ups at the table, a spicy Oktoberfest beer.

Whether I add leftover soup to the vegetables, or use leftover vegetables to make soup, I use up leftovers in ways that don't look or taste like, well, leftovers! Use this base recipe for potpie as a launching pad for your own creativity.

The crust is made from whole-wheat flour, which always includes the bran and the germ of the wheat. Its use is crucial for a full-flavored, robust pastry—just what the doctor ordered. With this crust, the healthful choice is the most flavorful. Imagine that!

continued

vegetable, mushroom, and chestnut potpie

continued

CRUST

I CUP UNSALTED BUTTER, FROZEN

2½ CUPS WHOLE-WHEAT FLOUR (with bran and germ)

¾ TEASPOON FINE SEA SALT

¼ TEASPOON BAKING POWDER

⅓ CUP ICE WATER

I. To make the crust, put 2 metal mixing bowls in the freezer for about 10 minutes. Remove 1 bowl and, using a box grater, vegetable peeler, or small knife, grate the butter into it. Return the bowl to the freezer.

2. Take the other bowl from the freezer and combine the flour, salt, and baking powder in it. Whisk several times to mix well.

3. Add the cold butter to the flour mixture and, using your thumbs and fore-fingers, a fork, or pastry blender, work the butter into the flour until the mixture resembles coarse cornmeal. Sprinkle the water over the mixture and mix with a large wooden fork or similar implement until the dough pulls away from the sides of the bowl and holds together.

4. Turn the dough out onto a lightly floured work surface and pat into a rough square about ¼ inch thick. Slide onto a baking sheet or flat plate, cover, and refrigerate for about 1 hour.

5. To make the pie filling, preheat the oven to 350°F.

6. Put the pearl onions in a bowl, drizzle with the grapeseed oil, and season with salt. Toss until evenly coated and then spread the onions on a baking sheet. Roast for about 15 minutes, or until lightly browned and beginning to soften. Remove from the oven and raise the temperature to 375°F.

7. While the onions are roasting, submerge the chestnuts in a saucepan of simmering water and cook for about 10 minutes. At this point, the thinner inside skin should come off with just a little prompting from a paring knife. Peel all the chestnuts and set aside.

PIE FILLING

8 OUNCES RED OR WHITE PEARL ONIONS, peeled

1 TABLESPOON GRAPESEED OR RICE OIL

FINE SEA SALT

18 CHESTNUTS, tough outer shells peeled (see Note)

4 CUPS LEFTOVER PUMPKIN SOUP WITH CRISPY SAGE GARNISH (page 41)

4 OUNCES COLLARD GREENS, stems removed and chopped

ABOUT 1½ CUPS (8 ounces) **LEFTOVER** HERB-ROASTED OVEN FRIES (page 128)

ABOUT 1½ CUPS (8 ounces) **LEFTOVER** SKILLET-BROWNED BROCCOLI AND CAULIFLOWER WITH PAN-TOASTED GARLIC (page 125)

ABOUT 1½ CUPS (8 ounces) **PEELED, LEFTOVER** CINNAMON-ROASTED SWEET POTATOES (page 124)

ABOUT 1 CUP (6 ounces) **LEFTOVER** ROSEMARY AND BALSAMIC PORTOBELLOS (page 129)

EXTRA-VIRGIN OLIVE OIL for serving

8. In a saucepan, bring the soup to a simmer over medium-high heat. Stir in the collard greens and cook until they collapse. Set aside, covered, to keep hot.

9. In a large bowl, combine the oven fries, broccoli and cauliflower, sweet potatoes, and portobellos. You may need to cut some of the vegetables so that they are all roughly the same size. Add the onions and chestnuts. Toss well and then transfer to a 9-inch square ceramic or glass baking dish. Everything should just fit.

10. Pour most of the soup and collards evenly over the vegetables. Dip a pastry brush into the remaining soup and lightly brush the rim of the dish. Pour the rest of the soup into the pie filling.

11. On a lightly floured work surface, roll the chilled dough into a square about 1 inch thick and about 1 inch larger than the baking dish on all sides.

12. Carefully lay the dough over the vegetables. (You may want to roll it around the rolling pin and then unroll it over the pie.) Pinch the dough along the sides of the dish to form a tight seal. Vent the crust in several places by making 1- to 2-inch slashes with a sharp knife.

13. Bake for 40 to 45 minutes, or until the crust is nicely browned and the filling is bubbling. Serve hot, and pass the olive oil for drizzling over each serving.

NOTE: For this recipe, you can use vacuum-packed peeled roasted chestnuts that you buy at specialty stores. Or, you can roast and peel chestnuts yourself. For instructions, see page 116.

CHAPTER
5

side dishes

LIKE SOUPS, SIDE DISHES ARE ENERGETIC CHEERLEADERS FOR THE SEASONS OF THE GARDEN. Everyone has a favorite vegetable, just as they have favorite sports teams. For some it's potatoes; for others, tomatoes or eggplants. Whatever your fancy, any vegetable is best enjoyed during its season because it is then at its peak of flavor. I prepare vegetables to celebrate this moment. Also, I try never to disguise the main attraction by mixing a number of vegetables together in the same dish. I focus only on one or two great vegetables that like each other, such as broccoli and cauliflower, and apply unexpected cooking techniques that take best advantage of the flavors. For instance, my SKILLET-BROWNED BROCCOLI AND CAULIFLOWER WITH PAN-TOASTED GARLIC (page 125) is a surefire way to renew an interest in both vegetables through the process of dry caramelization. The creamed corn recipe (page 133) hasn't a drop of cream but is nonetheless rich and creamy.

If you have leftover side dishes in the refrigerator, you will never go wanting for a meal. In my recipe for VEGETABLE, MUSHROOM, AND CHESTNUT POTPIE on page 117, I use the portobello mushrooms, the broccoli and cauliflower, and the pattypan squash from this chapter. The result? A rich and hearty mushroom and vegetable pie. It's not a giant leap to think of creative ways to use these vegetables as leftovers, which is important for the home cook with or without a growing family.

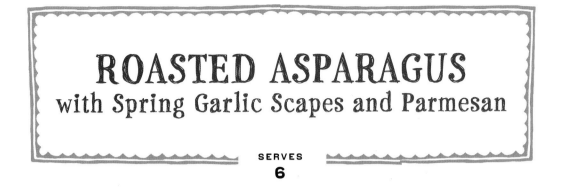

ROASTED ASPARAGUS
with Spring Garlic Scapes and Parmesan

SERVES
6

BECAUSE OF THE LIGHT FLAVORS AND PALE COLORS OF THE SPRING GARDEN, lots of folks think it's a wimpy season. Garlic scapes fly in the face of such blasphemy! These gray-green shoots, the tops of young garlic plants, are among the first arrivals in the garden, poking above the soil from the fall-planted garlic. They grow from the center of the plant, a graceful green stem that thickens on the end to form the seed head. Harvest them before they go to seed and you are in for a light but powerful blast of garlic flavor. The scapes don't have the pungency of mature garlic, but they sing with youthful exuberance when sautéed, grilled, or roasted. If you don't have them in your own garden, look for them at farmers' markets, where they are becoming increasingly popular.

FRESH GARLIC SCAPES,
each 6 to 10 inches long

2 TABLESPOONS GRAPESEED OR RICE OIL

SALT AND FRESHLY GROUND BLACK PEPPER

2 POUNDS ASPARAGUS

¼ CUP FRESHLY GRATED PARMESAN CHEESE

I. Preheat the oven to 400°F.

2. Divide the scapes in half. Lay one-half in a single layer on a baking sheet and drizzle with 1 tablespoon of the oil. Season lightly with salt and pepper.

3. Trim the tough ends from the asparagus, if necessary. Bend the stalks; they will break where they should be trimmed. (Young, spring asparagus should be very tender and may not need trimming.) Arrange the asparagus on top of the scapes, with the asparagus tips all facing in the same direction. Lay the rest of the scapes over the asparagus. Drizzle with the remaining oil and then scatter the cheese evenly over the top. Season again with salt and pepper.

4. Roast for 8 to 10 minutes, or until the asparagus begins to turn limp and the cheese is melted and browned. Slide onto a platter or transfer to the platter with a broad spatula. Serve right away.

Cinnamon-Roasted
SWEET POTATOES

SERVES 6

AS MUCH AS I LIKE TRADITIONAL PREPARATIONS MADE WITH SWEET POTATOES, they often include butter, brown sugar, and maple syrup—even marshmallows! Everyone knows these dishes. On their own, sweet potatoes are plenty sweet, so why add much more than a little local honey? Roasting them, as I do here, couldn't be easier, and the process accentuates the flavor of the tuberous root. I cut the potatoes in half, rub them with oil, and roast them alongside cinnamon sticks, which results in full-flavored sweet potatoes that melt on the tongue with plenty of natural sweetness.

Sweet potatoes are as easy to grow as any other kind of potato, but it's important to begin with organic seeds or starter potatoes from a reputable source. Once you try freshly dug potatoes of any color, you'll be sold. Take the kids with you when you dig them up—it's like finding buried treasure!

**2 TABLESPOONS
LOCAL HONEY**

**2 TABLESPOONS GRAPESEED
OR CANOLA OIL**

6 MEDIUM SWEET POTATOES,
unpeeled, halved lengthwise

**SALT AND FRESHLY GROUND
BLACK PEPPER**

6 CINNAMON STICKS

1. Preheat the oven to 375°F.

2. In a small bowl, whisk together the honey and oil. Rub the potato halves with this mixture and season with salt and pepper. Arrange, skin side down, in a shallow baking dish and bake for about 20 minutes, or until the potatoes begin to soften.

3. Remove the pan from the oven and turn the sweet potatoes skin side up. Tuck the cinnamon sticks under the potatoes. Roast for 20 to 30 minutes longer, or until the potatoes are cooked through and the cinnamon sticks are lightly browned.

4. Serve the sweet potatoes on a round platter with the browned cinnamon sticks bunched together and standing upright in the center of the platter.

Skillet-Browned
BROCCOLI and CAULIFLOWER
with Pan-Toasted Garlic

SERVES
6

VERY FEW PEOPLE ARE INDIFFERENT ABOUT BROCCOLI—they either love it or hate it! But whichever camp you are in, you will like it cooked this way. Caramelizing it in a hot skillet brings out broccoli's hidden deliciousness. The same is true of cauliflower. Truly! Both of these cruciferous vegetables are extremely nutritious, so finding new ways to cook them will be beneficial to a healthful diet.

There are two simple tricks that will guarantee success. One is to slice the broccoli and cauliflower thin enough so that they cook through by the time they brown and caramelize, yet they must be thick enough so they do not overcook. The second is to make certain the slices are the same thickness, guaranteeing they cook evenly. Otherwise, there's nothing to it! This recipe is another argument for keeping your cast-iron skillets front and center.

continued

skillet-browned broccoli and cauliflower with pan-toasted garlic

continued

I LARGE HEAD CAULIFLOWER, cored

2 TABLESPOONS GRAPESEED OR RICE OIL

SALT AND FRESHLY GROUND BLACK PEPPER

2 LARGE HEADS BROCCOLI, stems attached

2 TO 3 CLOVES GARLIC, thinly sliced

I TABLESPOON EXTRA-VIRGIN OLIVE OIL

I. Heat a large cast-iron skillet over medium heat. While it's heating, slice the cauliflower from top to bottom into 1-inch-thick slices. Brush both sides of every slice with some of the grapeseed oil and season with salt and pepper. Place the slices in the hot skillet, pressing them into the pan with a spatula. Cook for 3 to 4 minutes, or until nicely browned. Turn and cook on the other side for about 3 minutes, or until browned and tender. Transfer the slices to a warmed platter.

2. While the cauliflower is cooking, cut the broccoli the same way you cut the cauliflower and brush with some of the remaining grapeseed oil. When the cauliflower is cooked, cook the broccoli in the same way. Make sure both sides of the broccoli slices are browned before transferring the slices to the platter with the cauliflower.

3. Add the remaining grapeseed oil (about 2 teaspoons) to the hot skillet. Add the garlic slices and sauté, stirring gently and constantly, for 1 to 2 minutes, or until lightly browned. Transfer to a plate lined with paper towels and sprinkle with salt and pepper.

4. Arrange the broccoli around the outside of the platter and then put the cauliflower inside the circle. Sprinkle the toasted garlic slices over the broccoli and cauliflower, drizzle with the olive oil, and serve.

WATCH THE HEAT

I pay close attention to the intensity of the heat under my pots and pans when I cook. This holds for the grill, too, although monitoring its heat is more problematic. Blasting the heat is rarely the answer unless you are bringing liquid to a rapid boil or searing meat. Gentle heat works with delicate foods, such as fish and tender vegetables. Moderate heat works for most prolonged cooking. Read my recipes carefully to see how I adjust the heat up and down. Once you develop an awareness of the importance of heat variation in cooking, you'll be a better cook.

I often heat skillets on the burner before I add the oil. This may sound counterintuitive to some cooks. Shouldn't the oil heat along with the pan? I disagree. If you add the oil to a hot pan it will heat up quickly and there is less danger you will overheat the oil and release free radicals.

Herb-Roasted OVEN FRIES

SERVES
4

FRESHLY DUG POTATOES HAVE SO MUCH GOING FOR THEM IN TERMS OF TASTE AND TEXTURE, it's never easy to pinpoint only one attribute, but I especially like how beautifully they roast. They are so moist that after a short time in the oven, they are just perfect. Many cooks think first of frying, baking, or mashing potatoes, but these oven-roasted fries are excellent, particularly when made with fresh potatoes. I cut the potatoes into slices rather than wedges so that more of the surface comes into contact with the hot pan and the final result is crisp perfection. Be sure the pan is hot when you add the potatoes so that they sear immediately; you will have fewer incidences of burned potato sticking to the bottom of the pan. I weave herb stems among the potatoes for optimal flavor and to reduce the labor (no pulling leaves from the stems or chopping), and also because they make a great-looking garnish.

6 MEDIUM-LARGE YUKON GOLD POTATOES, cut into ½-inch-thick slices

GRAPESEED OR CANOLA OIL in a mister or spray bottle

SALT AND FRESHLY GROUND BLACK PEPPER

6 TO 8 FRESH ROSEMARY SPRIGS, about 3 inches long

6 FRESH SAGE SPRIGS, each with 3 to 5 leaves

1 SMALL YELLOW ONION, finely diced

1. Put a large cast-iron skillet in the oven and preheat the oven to 400°F.

2. In a large bowl, lightly mist the potatoes with oil, sprinkle with salt and pepper, and toss to mix.

3. Meanwhile, lightly spray the rosemary and sage sprigs with oil and set aside.

4. Remove the hot skillet from the oven and lay the potatoes in the skillet, arranging them in as close to a single layer as possible. Roast for about 15 minutes, or until the potatoes are browned on one side.

5. Turn the potatoes over and sprinkle evenly with the onion. "Weave" the rosemary and sage sprigs between the potatoes and return the skillet to the oven. Cook, turning the potatoes and herbs occasionally, for about 15 minutes longer, or until the potatoes are browned and cooked through.

6. Season the potatoes to taste with salt and pepper. Stack the potato slices, with the herbs between them, on a warmed platter and serve.

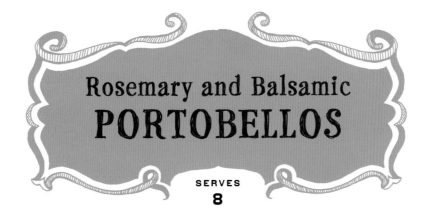

Rosemary and Balsamic
PORTOBELLOS

SERVES
8

EVERYONE LOVES THE IDEA OF COOKING WITH HERBS, but some cooks become timid or tentative when it comes time to add the herbs. Here's a simple and powerful way to flavor meaty portobello mushrooms with heady rosemary. No need to pick the spiky leaves from the stems—a job that, quite frankly, many folks never finish. Instead, cut long lengths from the rosemary plant (or buy them), lay the sprigs parallel to one another on a baking sheet, and set the mushrooms on top of them. The rosemary stems are an amazing and delicious garnish, plus the rosemary leaves don't get stuck in your teeth!

8 PORTOBELLO MUSHROOMS

¼ CUP BALSAMIC VINEGAR

GRAPESEED OR CANOLA OIL
in a mister or spray bottle

SALT AND FRESHLY GROUND BLACK PEPPER

4 LONG FRESH ROSEMARY SPRIGS

EXTRA-VIRGIN OLIVE OIL
for brushing

1. Preheat the oven to 400°F.

2. Remove the stems and gills from the portobello mushrooms and turn them, hollow side up, on a work surface. Sprinkle the mushrooms evenly with the balsamic vinegar, working gradually until it is all absorbed by the mushrooms. Lightly spray the mushrooms with grapeseed oil and season with salt and pepper.

3. Lay the rosemary sprigs parallel to one another on a baking sheet (like railroad tracks). Arrange the mushroom caps over the rosemary sprigs, creating 2 rows of 4 mushrooms each.

4. Roast for 5 minutes. Turn the mushrooms over and roast for 3 to 5 minutes longer, or until softened.

5. Transfer the mushrooms and rosemary to a warmed platter. Brush lightly with olive oil and drizzle with any juices in the pan. Serve warm or at room temperature.

Shiitake MUSHROOM and Koshihikari RICE CAKES

**SERVES
4**

WHAT AN AWESOME WAY TO COOK RICE. IT TAKES SOME EFFORT BUT, believe me, everyone who has tasted these flavorful little cakes just can't seem to get enough of them. Most of us simmer or steam rice, or bake it as pilaf, while others like to make risotto. If you are in the risotto camp, you have to try this recipe. The method is the same, but this offers a cross-cultural approach: Instead of Arborio rice, I use Koshihikari rice, a sticky, short-grain sushi rice; instead of wine, I use sake; instead of chicken stock, I use easy-to-make mushroom broth. I include the recipe in this chapter on sides, but these intensely flavored cakes make a great vegetarian main course, too.

I OUNCE DRIED SHIITAKE MUSHROOMS

4 OUNCES FRESH SHIITAKE MUSHROOMS, stemmed, with stems reserved and caps diced (about I¼ cups diced caps)

I½ CUPS WATER

¼ CUP MUSHROOM SOY SAUCE (see Note)

continued

I. In a mini processor, break up the dried mushrooms by pulsing once or twice. Or, use your fingers or kitchen shears to break up the dried mushrooms.

2. In a heatproof bowl or other heatproof container with a lid, combine the dried mushrooms and fresh mushroom stems. Reserve the diced fresh mushroom caps.

3. Bring the water to a boil and pour over the dried mushrooms and fresh stems to cover. Add more boiling water, if necessary. Cover tightly with aluminum foil or a lid and set aside for 30 minutes.

4. Pour the mushrooms and their liquid through a chinois or fine-mesh sieve into a saucepan. Press on the solids to extract as much liquid as possible. Discard the solids.

5. Set the saucepan over low heat and heat the mushroom liquid until hot but not simmering. Adjust the heat to its lowest setting to keep the liquid hot. Stir in the mushroom soy sauce.

continued

3 TABLESPOONS GRAPESEED OIL

¼ **CUP FINELY DICED SHALLOT**
or yellow onion

I **CUP KOSHIHIKARI** or other sushi rice

¾ **CUP SAKE**

¼ **CUP THINLY SLICED SCALLION,**
white and green parts

½ **CUP PANKO** (see Note)

**2 TABLESPOONS BLACK
SESAME SEEDS**

6. Heat 1 tablespoon of the oil in a heavy saucepan over medium-low heat until hot. Add the shallot and sauté for 1 to 2 minutes, or until translucent. Add the reserved diced fresh mushroom caps and sauté for 2 to 3 minutes, or until soft.

7. Add the rice and cook, stirring constantly with a wooden spoon, for about 2 minutes, or until the rice is hot and well mixed with the shallot and mushrooms, turns light golden, and smells toasty. Slowly add the sake and cook, stirring constantly, for 4 to 5 minutes, or until the sake is absorbed by the rice.

8. Add about one-third of the hot mushroom liquid and cook, stirring constantly with a wooden spoon, for 5 to 6 minutes, or until absorbed by the rice. Add the rest of the mushroom liquid and cook, stirring gently and constantly, for 7 to 8 minutes longer, or until the rice resembles thick risotto and any excess liquid is absorbed.

9. Transfer the rice to a square or rectangular baking dish large enough to spread it no deeper than 2 inches. Gently stir and fold the rice with the wooden spoon while it cools. This develops the strength of the rice so that you will be able to form rice cakes. Once the rice is cool to the touch, stir in the scallion. Cover and refrigerate for at least 1 hour or up to 6 hours.

10. Using 2- to 3-inch-diameter ring molds, form 8 rice cakes by firmly pressing the cold rice into the molds. The smaller rings will be filled to the top, the larger rings about two-thirds full.

11. Spread the panko on flat plate or tray and the sesame seeds on a second tray. Press one side of each rice cake in the panko and the other side in the sesame seeds. Gently push the rice cakes from the molds and arrange on a parchment-lined baking sheet or tray.

12. Heat 1 tablespoon of the remaining oil in each of 2 large, nonstick skillets over medium heat. Place 4 cakes, sesame seed side down, in each skillet, and cook for 3 minutes, or until darkened. Turn the cakes and cook for 3 minutes longer, or until evenly cooked. Serve warm or at room temperature.

NOTES: Mushroom soy sauce, a dark soy sauce flavored with mushrooms, is usually available in Asian markets or can be mail ordered (see Sources, page 221). Panko is coarse, Japanese-style bread crumbs sold in Asian markets and some supermarkets.

Vanilla "CREAM" CORN

SERVES 6 TO 8

I LEARNED A LOT ABOUT FLAVORS FROM MY MOM, who innately understood that if certain foods smelled good together, they would taste good together, too. Vanilla and corn are one such natural combination, and while my mother could not get fresh vanilla beans (in fact, she didn't even know about vanilla beans until later in her life), she used the best pure vanilla extract she could find in our suburban Illinois town. She stewed corn in cream and flavored the mixture with the vanilla and, believe me, it was awesome!

I set out to re-create her dish without the cream. Once I discovered that the juice from raw kernels thickened naturally, this was easy. I could make the cream corn I grew up loving, while giving a very firm nod to well-being. Because of its pure corn flavor, the naturally thickened corn juice is even better than the dish my mother prepared, and the vanilla adds a fantastic, mysterious flavor statement.

10 TO 12 MEDIUM TO LARGE EARS CORN, shucked

¼ CUP WHOLE MILK

1 FRESH VANILLA BEAN, split lengthwise, or ½ teaspoon pure vanilla extract

SALT AND FRESHLY GROUND BLACK PEPPER

1. Using a sharp knife, cut the corn kernels from the cobs. You should have 9 to 10 cups kernels. Discard the cobs.

2. Juice half the corn kernels in a heavy-duty juicer. Remove the pulp from the juicer and put it in a fine-mesh sieve. Press on the pulp to extract as much juice from it as you can. Combine this juice with the rest of the corn juice for a total of about 2 cups.

3. In a large saucepan, combine the corn juice, the remaining corn kernels, the milk, and the vanilla bean (if using extract, add later) and bring to a simmer over medium-low heat. Simmer gently, stirring constantly, for 2 to 3 minutes, or until the mixture begins to thicken. Simmer for about 3 minutes longer or until the corn is cooked through. If using extract, stir it in after the corn is cooked.

4. Season to taste with salt and pepper and serve immediately.

Grilled Red and Yellow
PEPPERS

SERVES
6

I LOVE FRESH BAY LEAVES AND HAPPILY THEY ARE SURPRISINGLY EASY TO GROW. The hand-some bay plant flourishes outside in the warm months and overwinters well in a cool, sunny spot indoors during the cold ones. This makes it a great candidate for year-round use to flavor preparations such as these peppers in the summertime and soups and stews all winter long.

Fire-grilled peppers and fresh bay leaves are an amazing combination. The subtle flavor of the bay leaves deepens the smoky sweetness of the peppers. While fresh bay leaves are edible, they are not meant to be eaten. Like their dried (and tasteless) counterparts, they should be removed before the dish is served. Unlike dried bay leaves, fresh ones can be reused in uncooked preparations such as this one.

3 LARGE RED BELL PEPPERS

3 LARGE YELLOW BELL PEPPERS

2 TABLESPOONS EXTRA-VIRGIN OLIVE OIL

½ TEASPOON SALT

¼ TEASPOON FRESHLY GROUND BLACK PEPPER

12 FRESH BAY LEAVES or basil leaves

1. Prepare a charcoal or gas grill for grilling over a medium-hot fire. Lightly oil the grill grate.

2. When the fire is ready, place the peppers over the hottest part of the fire and grill until they begin to char on the first side. Using tongs so that you don't puncture the peppers, continue to turn and grill the peppers until they are charred on all sides. Immediately transfer to a container just large enough to hold them, cover with plastic wrap, and set aside until cool enough to handle.

3. Peel the blackened skin from the peppers, using your fingers and scraping gently with a small knife. Cut the peppers in half, scrape out the seeds, and transfer the halves to a bowl.

4. Add the olive oil, salt, and pepper to the peppers and toss gently. If using basil leaves, thinly slice them. Slip the bay leaves or basil slices between the peppers so that each pepper half is in contact with the herb. Set aside for at least 1 hour. For longer storage, cover and refrigerate for up to 1 week.

5. Just before serving, remove the bay leaves, if used. Serve the peppers at room temperature.

Garden VEGETABLE and POTATO Lyonnaise

SERVES 6

WHEN I WAS LEARNING TO BE A CHEF, I LOVED THE TIME I SPENT WORKING IN FRENCH RESTAURANTS, largely because of how the French prepare potatoes: *pommes de terre Anna, pommes de terre dauphine,* and *pommes de terre à la lyonnaise* were some of my favorites. It is the humble but elegant Lyonnaise-style potato dish that inspired this gratin.

I use a variety of root vegetables as well as potatoes and layer them with the mandatory thinly sliced onions. The finished product is thicker than and not as crisp as the original, but the flavor is remarkable. The trick to success is to cook the gratin between two baking sheets so that both sides brown evenly and there is enough stability to turn the gratin halfway through baking. By the way, leftovers make a fantastically crisp breakfast dish, sautéed in extra-virgin olive oil and just a thumbnail of unsalted butter. Try them with eggs or on their own.

I TABLESPOON OLIVE OIL

SALT AND FRESHLY GROUND BLACK PEPPER

I RUTABAGA
(about 8 ounces), peeled

I SWEET POTATO
(about 8 ounces), peeled

2 SMALL TURNIPS
(about 12 ounces total), peeled

½ WHITE OR YELLOW ONION,
thinly sliced

3 YUKON GOLD POTATOES
(about 1¼ pounds total), peeled

1½ TABLESPOONS GRAPESEED OIL

I. Preheat the oven to 400°F. Have ready two 9-by-11-inch (or thereabouts) rimmed baking sheets. Lightly oil 1 baking sheet with half of the olive oil and sprinkle with salt and pepper.

2. Cut the rutabaga in half from top to bottom so that it fits the blade of a French or Japanese mandoline. Wearing a double layer of latex gloves to protect your slicing hand from the blade, cut the rutabaga into ⅛-inch-thick slices. Cut the sweet potato lengthwise into ⅛-inch-thick slices. Finally, cut the turnips into ⅛-inch-thick slices. Take care to keep each of the vegetables separate from the others.

3. Arrange slightly fewer than half of the rutabaga slices, overlapping them shingle fashion, in the prepared pan, covering the bottom completely. Arrange slightly fewer than half of the sweet potato slices, shingle fashion, evenly over the rutabaga slices. Sprinkle half of the onion slices over the sweet potato slices and then top with slightly fewer than half of the turnips.

4. Slice the potatoes as you need them to prevent them from browning. (Or, slice the potatoes all at once and keep them submerged in ice water to prevent browning.) Arrange a layer of potato slices, shingle fashion, over the turnips. Sprinkle with salt and pepper. Repeat the layering, saving enough of each vegetable so that the final layer can be a colorful combination of all of them.

5. Lightly pat the top layer with grapeseed oil and sprinkle with salt and pepper. Oil the bottom of the second baking sheet with the remaining olive oil and set directly on top of the gratin.

6. Wrap the baking sheets tightly and securely together with heavy-duty aluminum foil to hold the gratin firmly between them and to prevent leaking.

7. Bake for 25 minutes and remove from the oven. Wearing heavy oven mitts, carefully flip the pans holding the gratin. Be sure to keep a hand securely on the bottom baking sheet as you do this. Return the gratin to the oven and bake for 25 minutes longer.

8. Very carefully unwrap and discard the foil and let the gratin rest for about 5 minutes. Lift off the top baking sheet. Lay a large cutting board over the top of the gratin and, again wearing oven mitts, flip the gratin onto the cutting board. Carefully remove the second baking sheet. Slice the warm gratin into rectangle-shaped portions and serve at once.

Split-and-Grilled
SUMMER SQUASH
with Verbena-Onion Sauté

**SERVES
6**

IT'S NOT UNCOMMON TO BECOME BORED WITH SUMMER SQUASHES BY SEASON'S END—but it's not necessary either. I love grilled summer squashes prepared so that they stand very much on their own, rather than being relegated to the status of just another vegetable tossed in a casserole or ratatouille-style dish. I split and grill unadorned summer squashes and, after they get tender and take on a lovely smokiness, I serve them with a lemony onion sauce. This is a terrific side dish, but it could be a main course.

Some backyard cooks don't like to grill squashes because they find they take on a gray-ish color and off flavor. This is because they brush them with oil before grilling, which causes flare-ups and excess smoke and leaves a nasty aftertaste that mutes the delicate flavor of the squashes. All summer squash varieties possess natural viscous juices that help the vegetable cook on the grill without sticking. So, my advice: Don't oil the squash; oil the grill instead. Dip a kitchen towel in canola oil and rub it on a clean grill grate. When the grill is nice and hot and the grates appear dry, put the squash on the grill. This guarantees distinct, attractive grill marks.

2 SWEET ONIONS such as Vidalia or Walla Walla, cut into 1/4-inch-thick slices

2 TABLESPOONS RICE OR GRAPESEED OIL

SALT AND FRESHLY GROUND BLACK PEPPER

3 LARGE CLOVES GARLIC, thinly sliced

1/4 CUP LOOSELY PACKED FRESH LEMON VERBENA LEAVES

12 ASSORTED SMALL TO MEDIUM SUMMER SQUASHES such as pattypan, zucchini, and yellow crookneck (4 to 4 1/2 pounds total)

1. Prepare a charcoal or gas grill for grilling over a medium-hot fire. Lightly oil the grill grate.

2. Meanwhile, toss the onions with the oil and salt and pepper to taste.

3. Heat a large skillet over medium heat. When hot, add the onions and cook for 4 to 5 minutes, or until they begin to brown. Add the garlic and cook for 2 to 3 minutes longer, or until it begins to brown. Stir in the verbena leaves and immediately remove from the heat. Set aside and cover to keep warm. You will have about 2 cups onion mixture.

4. Split each squash in half lengthwise, or horizontally for pattypans, to preserve the original shape of the squash. Season the cut sides with salt and pepper.

5. When the fire is ready, place the squash, cut side down, on the hottest part of the grill and cook for about 2 minutes, or until you see clear grill marks when you lift the squash. Rotate each squash half a half-turn and grill for 2 to 3 minutes longer, or until marked with cross-hatching. Turn the squash halves over so that they are skin side down. Grill for about 3 minutes longer, or until the squash is just heated through.

6. Arrange the squash halves on a warmed serving platter and top with the verbena-onion sauté. Serve at once.

COUNTERTOP GRILLS

If you haven't invested in a countertop grill, such as a George Foreman grill or a panini grill, I suggest you wait no longer. They are not terribly expensive and are terrific for fast, fat-free cooking when you don't have time or the weather is not right for outdoor grilling. Lori and I love the grill for vegetables, meat, and poultry, and our kids love it for grilled sandwiches. Trust me, these grills are not just another gimmick. You will use yours over and over again once you start grilling food for good health and good flavor.

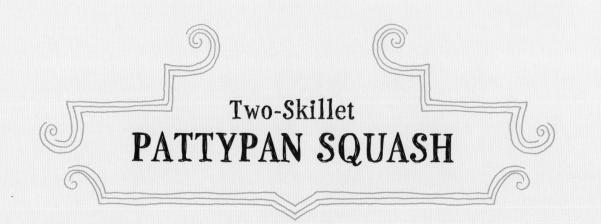

Two-Skillet
PATTYPAN SQUASH

SERVES
6

LIKE MANY HOBBY GARDENERS, I FIND MYSELF WITH A SURPLUS OF SUMMER SQUASHES come September. It's not as easy as you might think to give them away. Many people don't know quite what to do with them, while others wrongfully dismiss them as bland and insipid. Truth be told, a summer squash has a lovely, delicate flavor that only needs coaxing to reach its full glory. Steaming or blanching squashes won't do the trick, and so I turn to one of my favorite methods: cooking between two cast-iron skillets.

Consider the benefits of the controlled, even heat of the two skillets working in tandem to cook a beautiful summer squash such as pattypan. Put your favorite herbs in the hot pan, top them with the squashes, and then set the second skillet in place so that it presses on the squashes and ensures even caramelization and optimal flavor. Within ten short minutes you

have roasty-toasty silken squashes perfumed with the aromatic hint of the fresh herb and the crunchy snap of sea salt. Nothing insipid here!

THREE 8- TO 10-OUNCE
PATTYPAN SQUASHES
or equal-weight zucchini

1 TABLESPOON RICE
OR GRAPESEED OIL

COARSE SEA SALT

6 FRESH THYME SPRIGS

FRESHLY GROUND BLACK PEPPER

1 TEASPOON EXTRA-VIRGIN
OLIVE OIL

1. Pattypans look like flying saucers or bagels without a hole. With this in mind, it's easiest and safest to cut the pattypan like a bagel. Split it in half horizontally, trim the stem off, and if there is a navel (bump) on the bottom, trim it just so the bottom is level. Repeat with the other 2 squashes. If using zucchini, cut them in half lengthwise. Drizzle the rice oil over the cut side of each squash half.

2. Have ready 2 large cast-iron skillets, each one large enough to hold the halved squashes in a single layer if possible. Heat 1 skillet over medium-high heat. When the skillet is evenly hot, reduce the heat to medium and allow the skillet to sit on the heat until the heat of the pan is constant. Lightly sprinkle the salt over the bottom of the hot skillet.

3. Set a thyme sprig in the skillet where you will set each squash half. Put each squash half, cut side down, on top of a sprig. (You may have to cook the squashes in batches.) Immediately put the second skillet on top of the squash halves and press firmly for about 30 seconds. Cook for about 10 minutes, turning the bottom skillet a quarter turn every 2 minutes to ensure even browning.

4. Lift the top skillet off the squash halves. Turn the halves over and cook, without the second skillet, for about 2 minutes longer, or until tender to the touch.

5. Remove the pan from the heat and remove the squash halves from the pan. Season to taste with salt and pepper and drizzle each half with a little of the olive oil. Serve immediately with the thyme sprigs.

extending
the harvest

AS I HAVE EXPLAINED, I PLANTED THE GARDEN AS AN HOMAGE TO MY MOTHER. I wanted to do for my own kids what she had done for my brothers, my sister, and me by raising much of the food we eat. Growing up with a working, bountiful garden will teach my kids simple life lessons, I reasoned. But so much more happened once I started working in the garden: The floodgates of memory opened and nearly overwhelmed me. Believe me, there were a number of times during the first season when I was glad I was alone among the plants, so raw were my emotions.

Many of my recipes are quite different from my mom's, and so I don't think about her as often when I am in a restaurant kitchen or at home. But the minute I pull a Ball jar from the cupboard or notice that the leaves are changing color, I think about her. Mom loved to can fruits and vegetables to extend the harvest. During the first hot, humid days of school in late August and early September, when my brothers ran off to play football in the afternoon, I literally ran home to help my mom put up tomatoes or pickles. I could smell the fruits of her labor when I was three blocks away and couldn't wait to join her in the overheated, steamy kitchen. For me, nothing was cooler. She spoke of canning and preserving as a way to ensure that her family would have good, healthful food all winter. We could afford to buy food, of course, but Mom took special pride in her put-ups. They provided her with a sense of security: she knew the food was good and abundant, no matter what might happen. I know now this yearning for security came from her experiences growing up during the Great Depression, but it also allowed her to show us how much she loved us, loved food, and never wanted us to go to bed hungry or wanting.

I realize that my mother believed deeply in the same principles that those of us who believe in sustainability foster. When I am in the kitchen making the foods in this chapter, I know my mom and I are together, just like we used to be. I also know that everything is going to be just fine.

SUMMER PEACH
and Caramelized Onion Jam

MAKES
ABOUT **5** PINTS

A GOOD PEACH IS LIKE A GOOD TOMATO: When it's perfect, there's no reason to do much to it! The season when peaches are at their peak is short, so you want to find ways to use as many as you can. Because peaches love savory flavors, I developed this recipe for a luscious jam that includes caramelized onions. My mom knew that one way to get her kids to eat onions was to caramelize them, which makes them lose their bite and take on a mild sweetness. Pair them with briefly cooked peaches and you have a winner. The lemon verbena (see page 47) is a treat that is easier to grow than to find in the markets, and once you start planting it in the garden, you will savor its heady fragrance every time you work near it.

I like this jam spread on toast or crackers, served with grilled swordfish or tuna, or as an accompaniment to cheese. Cheese is by far my favorite dairy product for two reasons: Its natural flavor complexities and the cultures used to make it are healthful. You could make this jam with another stone fruit (plums, nectarines, or apricots), but peaches are my favorite. They make a powerful statement for nature's success at providing us with a near-perfect food.

continued

summer peach
and caramelized onion jam

continued

I TABLESPOON GRAPESEED OIL

I SWEET ONION such as Vidalia
or Walla Walla, cut into ¼-inch-thick slices

**FRESHLY GROUND BLACK
PEPPER**

**2 QUARTS SUPER-RIPE
PEACHES,** peeled, pitted, and cut into
eighths (about 12 peaches)

½ CUP WATER

**½ CUP FRESH LEMON VERBENA
LEAVES,** thinly sliced

6½ CUPS RAW CANE SUGAR

**I TO 2 TABLESPOONS
FRESH LEMON JUICE**

**2 TEASPOONS COARSE
SEA SALT**

I. In a large, nonstick skillet, heat the oil over medium-high heat. When hot, lay the onion slices in a single layer and cook for about 3 minutes, or until the bottom of the slices are brown. As the slices cook, rotate the pan by quarter turns at regular intervals to ensure even browning. Using a nonstick spatula, turn the slices over, sprinkle with pepper, and cook for 3 to 4 minutes longer, or until the onion slices are cooked through.

2. Meanwhile, in a large nonreactive saucepan, combine the peaches and water and bring to a simmer over medium-low heat. Cook for about 10 minutes, or until softened. Add the onion, lemon verbena, sugar, 1 tablespoon lemon juice, and the salt and simmer until the sugar dissolves.

3. Raise the heat to medium, bring to a boil, and cook for 8 to 10 minutes longer, or until thick. Skim any foam that rises to the surface, but take care not to remove too much of the liquid. Taste and add more lemon juice, if necessary.

4. See page 151 for instructions on sterilizing jars and lids and on processing the jam in a water bath. Ladle the peach mixture into sterilized pint jars, filling them to the base of the rim, then cover with lids and secure with screw-on rings.

5. Let cool and refrigerate for up to 3 weeks, or process in a water bath for 15 minutes, let cool, and store in a cool, dry place for up to 6 months.

BLUEBERRY, LEMON, and CHILI PEPPER JAM

MAKES
ABOUT **10** HALF-PINTS

WHEN I CREATE PRESERVES, I always try to push the flavor envelope by using unusual ingredients, such as chili peppers and salt. The result is a battery of savory jams that have a wider application than only as a topping for bread or a glaze for fruit tarts. In this recipe, the salt brings out the fruitiness, a trick I learned from a French chef with whom I trained. I recall thinking a weak *sauce bigarade* (orange sauce for duck) needed more orange juice and zest, but the chef told me to add the tiniest pinch of salt. It worked! Of course, you don't want to overdo it.

I appreciate the acidity and mineral qualities of blueberries, as well as their amazing health benefits, which have been touted for helping with memory and eyesight. Recent studies indicate that the powerful antioxidants in blueberries may help prevent certain types of cancer. So, why not eat them as often as possible? As I describe in more detail on page 215, my neighbor Bob Connelly grows scores of blueberry bushes, and we trade vegetables for berries, a neighborly relationship that works! My blueberry jam—indeed all my preserves—is looser and less sweet than most. I find many jams are so cloyingly sweet that the flavor of the fruit is diminished. Try this jam as a glaze for meat or poultry, spread it on bread or muffins, or use it on toast points schmeared with a little goat cheese. People will talk!

I CINNAMON STICK

3 PINTS BLUEBERRIES

2¼ CUPS RAW CANE SUGAR

¼ CUP JULIENNED
LEMON ZEST

I TABLESPOON SEEDED,
MINCED JALAPEÑO CHILI

SCANT I TEASPOON SALT

SCANT ½ TEASPOON SEEDED,
MINCED HABANERO CHILI

2 TABLESPOONS THINLY
SLICED FRESH CILANTRO
LEAVES AND STEMS

1. Holding the cinnamon stick with tongs, toast it an inch or so above a high gas flame for about 1 minute, or until it darkens a shade and is fragrant. You can also set it directly on a hot electric coil and turn it as it toasts. This takes 20 to 30 seconds. With either method, be sure to wear oven mitts or use a reliable pot holder. Set aside.

2. Mix the blueberries and sugar in a large nonreactive bowl and crush, using a fork or large spoon, until well mashed. Transfer to a large nonreactive saucepan.

3. Put the saucepan over medium-high heat and stir in the toasted cinnamon stick, lemon zest, jalapeño, salt, and habanero. Bring to a simmer, reduce the heat to low, and cook uncovered, stirring occasionally, for 30 to 40 minutes, or until thickened.

4. Remove the cinnamon stick, stir in the cilantro, and simmer for 1 minute.

5. See page 151 for instructions on sterilizing jars and lids and on processing the jam in a water bath. Ladle the blueberry mixture into sterilized half-pint jars, filling them to the base of the rim, then cover with lids and secure with screw-on rings.

6. Let cool and refrigerate for up to 3 weeks, or process in a water bath for 7 minutes, let cool, and store in a cool, dry place for up to 6 months.

STRAWBERRY, RHUBARB,
and Caramelized Onion Preserves

MAKES
ABOUT **3** PINTS

ONIONS, SALT, AND PEPPER WITH FRUIT? You bet! My mom frequently added salt and pepper to jams or desserts to intensify the good flavor of the ripe fruits. Small doses of black pepper are added to the French dessert *fraises aux poivre* to multiply the flavor of the strawberries (*fraises*). I take this concept a step further by relying on the aromatic quality of onions, which, as you may know, get sweeter the slower you cook them. In this recipe, the subtle flavor and aroma of the onion embrace the rhubarb and strawberries to create a long, sweet, and lasting finish. Serve the preserves with pork or chicken, with cheese, or spread on bread. Don't be afraid of canning these preserves. A water bath is simple to create and use, and the acid in the ingredients make these foolproof for canning.

I SMALL YELLOW OR WHITE ONION, cut into ¼-inch-thick slices (about I cup)

2 TEASPOONS GRAPESEED OR CANOLA OIL

I TO 2 FRESH RHUBARB STALKS, peeled and cut into ½-inch pieces (about I cup)

2 TEASPOONS LOCAL HONEY

½ CUP FRESH LEMON JUICE

3 CUPS RAW CANE SUGAR

I PINT STRAWBERRIES, hulled and halved (about 3 cups)

GRATED ZEST OF I LEMON

SALT AND FRESHLY GROUND BLACK PEPPER

I. In a small bowl, toss the onion with 1 teaspoon of the oil. In a second bowl, toss the rhubarb with the remaining 1 teaspoon oil.

2. Heat a sauté pan over medium heat. When hot, add the onion and sauté for 1 to 2 minutes, or until lightly browned. Add the rhubarb and cook for about 3 minutes longer, or until the rhubarb looks moist. Add the honey, raise the heat to medium-high, and cook, stirring constantly, for about 6 minutes, or until the rhubarb softens.

3. Add the lemon juice and sugar, raise the heat, and bring to a boil. Add the strawberries and lemon zest, reduce the heat to medium, and simmer for about 5 minutes, or until the berries have softened. Season with salt and pepper.

4. See facing page for instructions on sterilizing jars and lids and on processing the preserves in a water bath. Ladle the rhubarb-strawberry mixture into sterilized pint jars, filling them to the base of the rim, then cover with lids and secure with screw-on rings.

5. Let cool and refrigerate for up to 2 months, or process in a water bath for 20 minutes, let cool, and store in a cool, dry place for up to 6 months.

STERILIZING JARS AND LIDS
AND PROCESSING IN A WATER BATH

Lots of people are wary when they read a recipe that calls for processing a jam or other preserve in a water bath. For this reason, I always include the option of refrigerating the filled jars for a shorter period, usually at least a few weeks.

If you decide to take the plunge, so to speak, and use a water bath, begin by sterilizing the jars and lids. (You need to do this even if your efforts are headed straight to the refrigerator.) You will need canning jars, such as Ball or Mason jars, self-sealing lids, and screw-on metal ring bands. Submerge all of them in a pot of boiling water for about 5 minutes. Lift the jars from the boiling water with tongs and drain them on clean cloth towels. The lids and rings can sit in the water as it cools off the heat.

Next, fill the sterilized jars with the food. In the case of my recipes, this is usually a fruit or vegetable mixture that includes vinegar, citrus juice, and/or sugar, all of which promote safe storage. The jars should be filled just to the base of the rim, not to the very top. Do not wipe the jars clean around the rim, as the cloth can introduce bacteria. Instead, take care when you fill them to avoid drips.

Set the lids on the jars and screw them in place with the rings. At this point, use a clean, damp cloth to wipe any food from the outside of each jar. Bring a large, deep pot filled partway with water to a boil over high heat. Using tongs or a canning rack, submerge the jars in the water. Add more water if necessary to cover the jars by at least 2 inches. Let the water return to a boil before you begin timing, then boil according to the timing indicated in the recipe. Most jams and other preserves take 5 to 30 minutes.

Using tongs or the canning rack, lift the jars from the water. Your oven mitts will probably get wet, but canning is a watery process! Set the hot jars on the countertop—I usually cover the counter with a kitchen towel—and let them cool to room temperature. It is important that they not touch one another, so that air can circulate freely around them. The cooling can take 6 to 8 hours. I usually leave them overnight. As the jars cool, the lids will audibly pop and then indent slightly in the center. This is the sign of a good seal. When completely cool, unscrew the ring tops (they can be reused) and store the jars in a cool, dark place.

If the lid of a cooled jar has not sealed properly (the lid should be con- cave when pressed with a fingertip), the contents are still good. Simply store in the refrigerator and use within the time indicated in the recipe.

Citrus-and-Chili
PICKLED EGGPLANT

**MAKES
ABOUT 4 QUARTS**

I LOVE PICKLED EGGPLANT. It makes a great snack or condiment for smoked meats and fish, and is awesome added to marmalades, salsas, sandwiches, and tossed into vegetable salads. Well-tended eggplant plants produce a generous yield, and like so many gardeners, I am willing to give away only so much of my bumper crop. So, in late summer, I find myself in the kitchen pickling eggplants. Of course, I am never sorry to perform this task!

Here, I pickle small white Italian eggplants, but you could also use slender lavender Asian eggplants, dark purple Italian eggplants, or any heirloom variety you like to grow. I suggest that you gather together small, tender eggplants for pickling rather than very large ones. This recipe is unusual in that you need two large pots. I like bringing the brining liquid to a boil in one pot, which I then pour over the eggplants already cooking in another pot. This encourages the vegetable's flavors to develop fully. The very hot liquid returns to the boil very quickly, which keeps the pickled eggplants from being mushy.

4 POUNDS SMALL WHITE ITALIAN EGGPLANTS

2¾ CUPS WHITE WINE VINEGAR

3 TABLESPOONS COARSE SEA SALT

1½ TO 2 QUARTS WATER

3 OR 4 ORANGE ZEST STRIPS, each about 1 inch wide and 3 inches long

2 SMALL FRESH HOT CHILI PEPPERS such as habanero or jalapeño, halved and seeded

¼ CUP EXTRA-VIRGIN OLIVE OIL

4 LARGE CLOVES GARLIC, thinly sliced

2 TABLESPOONS GRATED LEMON ZEST

2 FRESH LEMON VERBENA SPRIGS, well dried

FINE SEA SALT AND FRESHLY CRACKED PEPPER

1. Trim the stem ends off the eggplants and cut them lengthwise into quarters.

2. Combine 2 cups of the vinegar and the salt in a large, nonreactive saucepan. Add enough of the water to cover the eggplant—the amount you need will depend on the size of the pan. Bring to a full boil over medium-high heat.

3. Heat another large saucepan over high heat. When the bottom of the pan is hot, add the eggplants and immediately pour the boiling vinegar mixture over them. Add the orange zest and chilies, bring to a boil, reduce the heat to medium, cover, and simmer for 15 to 20 minutes, or until the eggplants are tender. Drain the eggplants in a colander and discard the cooking liquid, orange zest, and chilies.

4. Select a bowl that will fit inside the colander. Fill the bowl with cool water and put this on top of the eggplants to press them lightly. Leave the bowl in place for about 2 minutes. Remove the bowl and lay the eggplants on wire cooling racks. Let cool for about 30 minutes to room temperature.

5. Using your fingers, peel the eggplants and remove any seeds, and then cut the flesh into ½-inch cubes. Transfer the cubes to a glass bowl.

6. Add the remaining ¾ cup vinegar, the olive oil, garlic, lemon zest, and lemon verbena. Toss well, cover, and refrigerate for 2 days. Taste and adjust the seasoning with sea salt and pepper.

7. Store the pickle in a tightly covered container in the refrigerator for up to 1 month.

CRANBERRY and CARAMELIZED ONION Sauce

MAKES
ABOUT **2** CUPS

WHEN FALL ARRIVES IN ALL ITS VIBRANT MAGNIF-ICENCE, I get ready for cranberries. I live in New England, so it's easy to find fresh cranberries in farmers' markets even before they show up in supermarkets. They grow in low-lying bogs and coastal regions in the Northeast, the Northwest, and the Great Lakes region. I can't emphasize how much better it is to buy them fresh, rather than processed in excessively sweet sauces, relishes, and juices. When you make sauces and other condiments with fresh berries, the texture and flavor is better by miles! Whatever you do, don't reserve cranberries only for Thanksgiving.

Celebrate the tiny, tart berry for its culinary versatility and its impressive health benefits. Research shows it's one of the most potent antioxidant fruits commonly eaten by Americans, which means cranberries can be powerful allies in the fight against heart disease and cancer.

They also fight food-borne pathogens and contain antibacterial properties. Recent studies have actually proven the old wives' tale that cranberries can prevent urinary tract infections. Eat them only once a year? I don't think so!

This condiment is made with caramelized onions, one of my favorite ways to add sweetness to a dish. I also sweeten the berries with apple juice, orange juice, and a little honey. This is plenty sweet for the kids, and if you're concerned about the wine, don't be. Much of the alcohol burns off and leaves only a lovely, subtle flavor behind. The most obvious way to serve this sauce is alongside a holiday turkey, but it's also fantastic served with ham, pork chops, or roast chicken. You can also use it as a glaze for pork, chicken, or goose, or stir it into pan gravies, add it to vinaigrettes, spread it on toast, and toss it with salads.

continued

cranberry and caramelized onion sauce

continued

2 CUPS CRANBERRIES

2 CUPS FRESHLY PRESSED APPLE JUICE or apple cider

I CUP FRESH ORANGE JUICE

I CUP DRY RIESLING WINE

2 CINNAMON STICKS

I TEASPOON LOCAL HONEY, plus more if needed

2 TABLESPOONS GRAPESEED OR CANOLA OIL

I YELLOW OR WHITE ONION, thinly sliced

SALT AND FRESHLY GROUND BLACK PEPPER

I. In a large, nonreactive saucepan, combine the cranberries, apple juice, orange juice, Riesling, and cinnamon sticks and bring to a slow boil over medium heat. Reduce the heat to low, cover, and simmer gently for 7 to 8 minutes, or until the cranberries soften and some pop open. Taste the cranberries and sweeten with a little honey if they are too tart. Cover and set aside to keep warm.

2. In a sauté pan, heat the oil over medium heat until it ripples, which indicates it's hot. Add the 1 teaspoon honey and the onion slices, sprinkle with salt and pepper, and cook, stirring occasionally, for 6 to 8 minutes, or until translucent and browned.

3. Add the onion to the cranberries, mix well, and taste and adjust the seasoning with salt, pepper, and more honey, if necessary. Serve warm or at room temperature. To store, spoon into a plastic or glass container, cover tightly, and refrigerate for up to 3 days.

TOMATO, BUTTER, and HONEY JAM

MAKES
ABOUT 2½ CUPS

I CALL THIS JAM BECAUSE IT'S FANTASTIC SPREAD ON WARM CORN BREAD, biscuits, scones, and dinner rolls. You can also swirl it into pan sauces for fish, pork, and chicken. It doesn't last as long as jams processed in a water bath or those with a lot of added sugar, but it will keep in the refrigerator for up to a week. Once you taste it, you will discover many uses for it, and it's an easy and tasty way to use summer's best tomatoes. Store it in glass or plastic.

2 POUNDS SUPER-RIPE TOMATOES (2 or 3 large tomatoes)

I TABLESPOON GRAPESEED OR RICE OIL

I SMALL YELLOW ONION, chopped

½ CUP CHILLED UNSALTED BUTTER, cut into ¼-inch-thick pats

¼ CUP LOCAL HONEY

2 TABLESPOONS FRESH THYME LEAVES

SALT AND FRESHLY GROUND BLACK PEPPER

¼ CUP LOOSELY PACKED, TORN FRESH BASIL LEAVES

I. Core the tomatoes and cut in half through the equator. One at a time, hold the tomato halves over a glass bowl and gently squeeze to remove the seeds and juice. Reserve the juice and seeds. Finely chop the tomato halves with a sharp knife, or process in a food processor until diced but not smooth or puréed. Set aside.

2. In a large, nonstick skillet, heat the oil over low heat. Add the onion and cook for about 5 minutes, or until translucent but not browned. Add the reserved tomato juice and seeds and the butter, raise the heat to medium, and simmer until the juice and butter form a thick sauce. Add the diced tomatoes, raise the heat, and simmer rapidly, stirring often, for about 20 minutes, or until thickened and saucy.

3. Remove the pan from the heat and stir in the honey and thyme and season to taste with salt and pepper. Set aside to cool to room temperature.

4. Stir in the basil and transfer the jam to a lidded container. Refrigerate and stir 2 or 3 times during chilling. Stir it one final time when completely cold. Let the jam come to room temperature before serving to give the butter time to soften.

PICKLED BANANA PEPPERS

**MAKES AS MANY QUARTS
AS YOU CAN**

MANY GARDENERS AND CHEFS USE THE NOBLE TOMATO TO EXPLAIN the ripening process and how critical it is for the best flavor and texture. But believe it or not, my first memory of "getting it" was with a banana pepper. As a child, I had no particular love for these peppers, but I remember watching them grow when I was five or six years old and begging my mother to let me pick them. They were the coolest shape! This was a daily—sometimes hourly—struggle between my mother and me, as I recall asking her over and over if I could pick the peppers. She patiently explained they were not the "right color" yet, and she also showed me how to get near the plant and smell the fruits. The morning finally came when the pale green peppers had turned bright yellow and my mom let me pick them. I remember smelling them and even as a child noting that the mild peppery aroma had turned marvelously smoky and leathery.

I didn't remember any of this until one day when my son, Ethan, who was then three years old, asked to pick some of the banana peppers he had patiently been watching ripen in the garden. When we snipped a few from the plant, he immediately put one to his nose and sniffed. "Oooh! These are smelling," he proclaimed with three-year-old pleasure. The memories of my mother's tender lesson flooded over me and I raced into the house to write this recipe and this note. To do the recipe justice, I decided to write it as my mother would have: no exact measurements but commonsense instructions that assume the reader has cooked before. For those who would like a little more guidance, I have provided approximate measurements, too.

1 CINNAMON STICK per quart jar

A WHOLE BUNCH OF BANANA PEPPERS (4 to 6 peppers per quart jar)

1 FENNEL HEAD (flower at full seed) **PER QUART JAR** (or 1 scant teaspoon fennel seeds per quart jar)

EQUAL PARTS WATER AND HONEY, enough to fill your jars (1 quart jar will require about 2 to 2½ cups honey water)

ENOUGH CIDER VINEGAR TO MAKE THE HONEY WATER TANGY (about 1 cup cider vinegar for every 2 cups honey water)

ENOUGH COARSE SEA SALT TO MAKE THE BRINE A LITTLE SALTY (about 1½ teaspoons per quart)

ABOUT 2 TEASPOONS GROUND TURMERIC PER QUART OF LIQUID (about 1 teaspoon per quart jar)

1. Holding the cinnamon sticks with tongs, toast them an inch or so above a high gas flame for about 1 minute, or until they darken a shade and are fragrant. You can also set them directly on a hot electric coil and turn them as they toast. This takes 20 to 30 seconds. With either method, be sure to wear oven mitts or use a reliable pot holder. Set aside.

2. See page 151 for instructions on sterilizing jars and lids and on processing the peppers in a water bath. Cut a slit in each in each pepper from stem to tip. This will allow the cooking liquid to enter the peppers. Remove the stems and, if you prefer milder peppers, scrape out the seeds. Put 1 cinnamon stick and 1 fennel head at the bottom of each jar and then pack the peppers uniformly into the jars, making sure they are at least 1 inch below the rim of the jar. Do not pack too tightly or the liquid will not enter some of the peppers.

3. In a nonreactive saucepan, bring the honey water, vinegar, salt, and turmeric to a full boil over high heat. Ladle enough of the mixture over the peppers in 1 jar to cover them by ½ inch. Cover with a lid and secure with a screw-on ring.

4. Fill the second jar the same way. Repeat this process until all the jars are filled. For the seal to be good, it is crucial that you return the mixture to a boil each time before you fill a jar and that you seal the jar the moment it is filled.

5. Wait for the lids to indent to prove the seal, then store in a cool, dark cupboard for up to 6 months. In the event the lids do not indent in 2 hours' time, process the jars in a water bath for 10 minutes. Store any jars that still do not indent (or if you decide to skip the water bath) in the refrigerator and consume the pickles within 6 weeks.

VEGETABLE MARMALADE

MAKES
ABOUT **5** PINTS

THIS RECIPE MAKES GOOD USE OF LEFTOVER GRILLED EGGPLANT AND LEFTOVER COOKED SQUASH, although you could start with fresh produce instead and cook it to order. You could also use leftover cauliflower, broccoli, or even Brussels sprouts, or you can toss in some cubes of raw winter squash during the last 20 minutes of cooking. You get the idea! Dried tomatoes are a must here. If you haven't oven dried them following my instructions on the facing page, you can substitute meaty sun-dried tomatoes from a good store. The results may not be quite as good.

What turns this recipe into a marmalade for me is not the addition of traditional citrus fruit, but the use of apple juice and plum juice. Both juices provide the necessary acid and are high in natural pectin to thicken the marmalade, so you don't need to add sugar.

6 QUARTS FRESHLY PRESSED APPLE JUICE or apple cider

2 QUARTS FRESH PLUM JUICE or more apple juice

I SMALL YELLOW ONION, quartered through the stem end

I½ CUPS CUBED LEFTOVER GRILLED EGGPLANT

I½ CUPS CUBED LEFTOVER TWO-SKILLET PATTYPAN SQUASH (page 140)

I½ CUPS SEMIDRY OVEN-DRIED TOMATOES (facing page)

I½ CUPS DICED GRILLED OR ROASTED ONIONS

2 TABLESPOONS GRATED LEMON ZEST or ¼ cup grated orange zest

3 CLOVES GARLIC, thinly sliced

I. Divide the apple juice and plum juice evenly between two 6-quart stockpots. Add 2 onion quarters to each pot. Bring to a simmer over low heat. Cook for 3 to 4 hours, or until reduced to 4 quarts total.

2. Combine the liquid in a single pot. Add the eggplant, squash, tomatoes, diced onion, citrus zest, and garlic. Return to a simmer and cook for about 5 minutes, or until heated through and blended.

3. See page 151 for instructions on sterilizing jars and lids. Ladle the vegetable mixture into sterilized pint jars, filling them to the base of the rim, then cover with lids and secure with screw-on rings. Let cool to room temperature and refrigerate for up to 6 weeks.

Oven-Dried TOMATOES

MAKES ABOUT **6** CUPS SEMIDRY,
OR **9** CUPS FULLY DRY

DRYING FOOD IS ONE OF THE MOST INGENIOUS AND ANCIENT METHODS FOR EXTENDING THE HARVEST. It's a sustainable, effective technique that relies on nothing more high-tech than consecutive days of dry, sunny weather, which of course means it works best in fairly arid climates. I live in Connecticut where the average rainfall is anywhere from forty-three to forty-eight inches a year, and so while I may dream about drying tomatoes on stone walls in the sunshine, I have to be realistic and use my oven. I imagine this is true for most of my readers.

For success, you need only a couple of wire cake cooling racks or mesh roasting racks to provide good air circulation. The simplest method calls only for low heat and salt: Low heat to dry without burning and salt to aid in the evaporation and act as a preservative. I mist the tomatoes with vinegar, and you could also season them with black pepper, green fennel seeds from the garden, dill seeds, or even garam masala. But the salt is crucial.

I dry some of my tomatoes to the semidry stage. They remain a little syrupy and keep only for a month packed in oil. Others I dry all the way, without oil, and store in airtight plastic bags or lidded glass jars. Either way, I use these all the time as fall and winter progress, and I count myself lucky if I have any left over by spring!

continued

oven-dried tomatoes

continued

BALSAMIC VINEGAR

8 POUNDS MEATY TOMATOES
such as Roma, Cherokee Purple, or
Brandywine

COARSE SEA SALT

1. Pour the vinegar into a mister or spray bottle.

2. Cover the bottom oven rack with aluminum foil or put a large rimmed baking sheet on it. Position it as low as possible in the oven. Position the second oven rack in the center of the oven. Preheat the oven to the lowest setting, either 150° or 200°F, depending on your oven.

3. Core the tomatoes (and compost the stem ends). If using plum tomatoes, cut each one in half lengthwise. Slice round tomatoes in half through the equator.

4. Mist the tomatoes lightly with the vinegar and sprinkle the cut sides evenly with salt.

5. Arrange the tomatoes, cut side up and side by side, on wire cooling racks. Do not let them touch. Put the cooling racks directly on the upper oven rack for maximum air and heat circulation. Let the tomatoes dry for 6 to 8 hours for semidry tomatoes, 10 to 12 hours for fully dry tomatoes. Check the tomatoes continually. Some will dry more quickly than others, depending on the moisture content and size of the tomato (yes, even tomatoes are individuals!). Remove them when they reach the desired dryness.

6. To store, refrigerate the semidry tomatoes in olive oil to cover for up to 1 month. Put the dry tomatoes in oil to cover or, without oil, in a zippered plastic bag or in a jar with a tight-fitting lid for up to 1 month.

TOMATO, BANANA PEPPER, and POLE BEAN SALSA

MAKES
ABOUT **2** QUARTS

THERE ARE LITERALLY THOUSANDS OF WAYS TO MAKE SALSA, and salsa recipes are one of the best ways to use up a variety of the vegetables you grow in the garden—peppers in particular. I plant a lot of pepper and chili plants because they are attractive, easy to grow, endlessly versatile in the kitchen, and nearly everyone loves them. Plus, hot chilies dry easily and can be used all winter long to add a little fire to any number of dishes. Here, I forgo the heat and work with mild yellow banana or Cubanelle peppers. These long, slender peppers sport big pepper flavor without the eye-watering punch that tends to scare some folks away. Cubanelles are greener than yellow banana peppers, but both taste and behave alike.

In this salsa, I mix the peppers with tomatoes and beans. If you have purple or yellow beans as well as green, I suggest mixing them for their colors. A word of caution: While I like to blanch the beans so that they retain their crunch, purple beans fade to a dull green when cooked, so leave them raw. Both the beans and the peppers give this salsa crisp texture and make it a winner paired with chips, fish, chicken, and pork. Change the type of zest if you think orange or lemon zest would taste better with your meal than lime zest.

2 POUNDS SUPER-RIPE TOMATOES

3 SCALLIONS

I POUND ASSORTED POLE BEANS
such as purple, yellow wax, and/or green,
in any combination

**4 BANANA OR CUBANELLE
PEPPERS,** seeded and chopped

**¼ CUP LOOSELY PACKED,
SLICED FRESH CILANTRO LEAVES
AND STEMS**

**2 TABLESPOONS ROASTED
GARLIC PASTE** (see Note)

GRATED ZEST OF 2 LIMES

**SALT AND FRESHLY GROUND
BLACK PEPPER**

¼ CUP FRESH LIME JUICE
(from about I lime)

I. Core the tomatoes and cut in half through the equator. Hold the tomato halves over a glass bowl and gently squeeze to remove the seeds and juice. Reserve the juice and seeds. Chop the tomato halves with a sharp knife into small dice. Thinly slice the scallions, both white and green parts, on the diagonal. Set the vegetables aside separately.

2. Trim the stem ends of the beans and strings any that need it. Bring a large saucepan filled with water to a boil. Add the green and/or wax beans and cook for 1 minute, or until crisp-tender. Remember, do not add purple beans, if using, as they will turn green in the boiling water. Check for doneness by removing a bean with a pair of tongs and sampling it. Drain the beans and plunge them into salted ice water to shock and stop the cooking. When the beans are well chilled, drain and press gently between cloth or paper towels to remove any excess water. Slice all the beans, including any raw purple ones, into pieces about the same size as the tomatoes and peppers. They will become wonderfully crunchy surprises in the mix and will also add their bright color.

3. In a nonreactive bowl, combine the tomatoes, reserved, tomato juice and seeds, scallions, beans, and peppers. Add the cilantro, garlic paste, and lime zest. Stir until well mixed and season to taste with salt and pepper. Season with the lime juice just before serving.

NOTE: To make roasted garlic paste, put unpeeled garlic cloves in a dry cast-iron skillet and cook over low heat, turning the cloves frequently so they soften but do not brown, for 20 to 30 minutes, or until softened. Slide the cloves from the skillet onto a plate to cool to the touch. Squeeze the softened garlic pulp from the individual cloves.

Homemade
APPLESAUCE

**MAKES
ABOUT 2 CUPS**

AS I TRAVEL AROUND THE COUNTRY TALKING TO PEOPLE ABOUT COOKING FOR WELL-BEING, many folks tell me they have started eating more applesauce and adding it to baking recipes. This is great and I applaud all efforts to eat more healthfully, but what most people don't realize is that many jars of commercially sold applesauce are laden with sugar or high-fructose corn syrup, or both. Luckily, making your own is easy and you can be sure it's good for you.

Fall is naturally the best time to make homemade applesauce because that's when you can get really good local apples. Good apples are key. I don't want to make your life difficult by calling for specific varieties, but it is well worth it to seek out the freshest, firmest, best available, preferably grown in your own backyard. Failing that, go to a local orchard and pick your own. It is fun and you know the fruit is fresh.

Plus, taking the kids to a pick-your-own orchard on a crisp fall day creates lasting family memories. Next best is to buy apples from farm stands and farmers' markets, or look for local apples in supermarkets, many of which are trying hard to connect with nearby farmers for some produce.

So many apple varieties exist, some experts think codifying them is almost futile. Buy the apples that taste best and your applesauce will taste so good that it won't need sweetening. If you decide you want a little sweetness, drizzle on local honey—another product available nearly everywhere in the country. Look for it at the same farm stand where you buy the apples.

2 CINNAMON STICKS

**2 POUNDS COX'S, ORANGE PIPPIN,
GRANNY SMITH, OR OTHER TART
APPLES**, peeled, cored, and sliced
(see Note)

**2 TABLESPOONS FRESH
LEMON JUICE**

1 TEASPOON FINE SEA SALT

1. Holding the cinnamon sticks with tongs, toast them an inch or so above a high gas flame for about 1 minute, or until they darken a shade and are fragrant. You can also set them directly on a hot electric coil and turn them as they toast. This takes 20 to 30 seconds. With either method, be sure to wear oven mitts or use a reliable pot holder. Set aside.

2. Juice 3 cups of the apples in a heavy-duty juicer. You will have about ⅔ cup juice and ⅓ to ½ cup pulp. In a nonreactive saucepan, combine the remaining apples, the juice and pulp, cinnamon sticks, lemon juice, and salt and bring to a simmer over medium heat. Reduce the heat to low, cover partially, and cook, stirring often, for about 30 minutes, or until the apples are tender and have broken down to a saucelike consistency.

3. Remove the cinnamon sticks. If you prefer a very smooth sauce and this one is not there yet, transfer it to a food processor and process until it reaches the desired consistency.

4. Serve the applesauce warm or at room temperature. It keeps very well, covered and refrigerated, for 2 to 3 days.

NOTES: If you don't have a juicer, use ⅔ cup freshly pressed apple juice or apple cider and only 1¼ pounds apples. For sweet applesauce, increase the total weight of the apples by 4 ounces, and then mix in ¼ cup local honey once the sauce is smooth.

HEIRLOOM TOMATO and EGGPLANT SAUCE

MAKES
ABOUT 2½ QUARTS

WOULDN'T IT BE GREAT TO RETURN TO THE DAYS WHEN everyone in the neighborhood argued about who made the best tomato sauce—and in order to "prove" one claim or the other, everyone got together to eat a simple meal? Let this sauce be the first step!

Homemade tomato sauce is more than just a topping for pasta. As good as it is for that very reason, it will enliven casseroles and chicken, meat, and fish dishes all winter long if it's properly frozen. It's also a way for individual cooks to express their culinary personalities, and to assure themselves that their families are getting only the most wholesome ingredients. This recipe reflects my particular personality in the kitchen. I adore all root vegetables, so I use turnips and rutabagas in place of the more traditional carrots. I also rely on cooked eggplant to thicken the sauce and give it a silken texture.

I like to cook the eggplant in a panini grill or other countertop grill (such as a George Foreman grill) because such grills don't require oil and the eggplant dries nicely as it cooks, which kick-starts its thickening power. A standard backyard grill or ridged stove-top grill pan works just fine, too, as does using leftover cooked eggplant. Take a lead from me and mix and match your own favorite vegetables in a versatile tomato sauce that celebrates your particular tastes and preferences. And let the contests begin!

**2 POUNDS ITALIAN OR
YOUR FAVORITE EGGPLANT,**
peeled and thickly sliced

¼ CUP GRAPESEED OR RICE OIL

**2½ CUPS CHOPPED YELLOW
ONION**

1 CUP CHOPPED TURNIP
(about 7 ounces)

½ CUP CHOPPED RUTABAGA
(about 3 ounces)

3 OR 4 CLOVES GARLIC,
finely chopped

8 CUPS CHOPPED TOMATOES
(about 4 pounds)

2 FRESH OREGANO SPRIGS,
each about 6 inches long

¼ CUP EXTRA-VIRGIN OLIVE OIL

**SALT AND FRESHLY GROUND
BLACK PEPPER**

**½ CUP LOOSELY PACKED, SLICED
FRESH BASIL LEAVES**

1. Prepare a charcoal or gas grill for grilling over a medium-hot fire. Lightly oil the grill grate.

2. When the fire is ready, place the eggplant slices over the hottest part of the fire and cook, turning once, for about 10 minutes total, or until softened. Alternatively, grill them on a countertop grill or in a ridged griddle pan on the stove top. Let the eggplant slices cool slightly and then chop into chunks. You should have about 2¼ cups eggplant. Set aside.

3. In a large, heavy-bottomed saucepan, heat the grapeseed oil over medium-high heat. Add the onion, turnip, and rutabaga and sauté for 3 minutes, or until the vegetables begin to soften. Cover with a tight-fitting lid and reduce the heat to medium. Cook, stirring occasionally, for 8 to 10 minutes, or until the vegetables are tender and browned. Add the garlic, reduce the heat to low, and cook, stirring occasionally, for about 7 minutes longer, or until cooked through.

4. Add the tomatoes, cooked eggplant, oregano, and olive oil. Bring to a full simmer, reduce the heat to medium-low, cover, and cook for 10 minutes. Remove and discard the oregano sprigs and continue to simmer, uncovered, for about 10 minutes, or until the flavors meld. Season to taste with salt and pepper, then stir in the basil. Use immediately or let cool completely.

5. When cool, cover and refrigerate overnight. Use within a day or two. To freeze, transfer the cooled sauce to plastic pint containers or zippered freezer bags and freeze for up to 6 months.

OLIVE OIL
Infused with Sage and Tarragon

MAKES
ABOUT 3 CUPS

HERE IS A GREAT WAY TO USE THE SAGE AND TARRAGON GROWING IN THE GARDEN or for sale in the farmers' market. A bunch is just that: What you can hold in your hand comfortably but generously. Use this infusion as a marinade, in salad dressings, tossed with pasta, or drizzled over sautéed fish or chicken. It's also a perfect dip for fresh bread.

3½ CUPS EXTRA-VIRGIN
OLIVE OIL

2 CINNAMON STICKS

6 GREEN CARDAMOM PODS

4 ORANGE ZEST STRIPS

I BUNCH FRESH SAGE

I BUNCH FRESH TARRAGON

1. In a saucepan, combine the oil, cinnamon sticks, cardamom, zest strips, half the sage, and half the tarragon over low heat until the oil reaches 100°F on a deep-fat thermometer. Maintain this temperature for 1 hour, monitoring it with the thermometer.

2. Strain the oil through a fine-mesh sieve into a bowl. Reserve the cardamom, orange zest strips, and cinnamon sticks; discard the sage and tarragon. Let the oil cool to room temperature.

3. Put the cinnamon, cardamom, orange zest strips, and the remaining sage and tarragon into a decorative 1-quart glass bottle.

4. Set a funnel in the bottle, pour in the oil, and seal tightly with a cork or cap. It will keep for up to 1 month in the refrigerator or at room temperature for up to 1 week.

Lavender, Ginger, and
ROASTED CHILI OIL

MAKES
ABOUT 1 QUART

HOT, SPICY OILS ARE GREAT TO HAVE AROUND to jazz up salad dressings, pasta dishes, and marinades. I like to dip bread into them, too. This one is designed to use the peppers and hot chilies I grow in the garden. If you grow lavender because it smells so good and looks so pretty, here's a nice way to use it in a culinary preparation. Don't worry if the lavender does not have flowers on it. The leaves and stems provide lovely flavor.

2 CUBANELLE OR BANANA PEPPERS

4 HABANERO OR JALAPEÑO CHILIES

2 TABLESPOONS GRAPESEED OR RICE OIL

4-OUNCE PIECE FRESH GINGER, peeled and thinly sliced (about ¾ cup)

3¼ CUPS GRAPESEED OR EXTRA-VIRGIN OLIVE OIL

1 OR 2 GENEROUS FRESH LAVENDER SPRIGS, with or without blossoms

1. Roast the Cubanelle and habanero peppers on a charcoal or gas grill, under the broiler, or over a gas flame until the skins blister and brown, then let cool to the touch (see the note accompanying OSAKA MUSTARD GREENS SALAD on page 25).

2. Wearing latex gloves (advisable because the peppers can irritate your skin), split each pepper in half lengthwise. Remove and discard the seeds.

3. Heat a deep saucepan or sauté pan over medium-high heat. When hot, add the 2 tablespoons grapeseed or rice oil. When the oil is hot, add the ginger and sauté for about 2 minutes, or until the edges curl slightly and the slices darken to yellow.

4. Add the pepper halves and cook for 1 minute, stirring. Stand back. The steam from the pot is peppery and can irritate your eyes. Slowly pour the 3¼ cups grapeseed or olive oil over the ingredients in the pan. When all of the oil is in the pan, cook for about 2 minutes, or until the oil starts to bubble. Continue to cook for 30 seconds and then remove from the heat and set aside to cool completely. Take great care; the oil is extremely hot.

5. When the oil is cool, use a slotted spoon to transfer the ginger and peppers to a 1-quart glass bottle or jar. Trim the lavender so that the sprigs will fit in the bottle just below the neck. Insert the lavender into the bottle.

6. Set a funnel in the bottle, pour in the oil, and seal tightly with a cork or cap. The chili oil will keep for up to 1 month in the refrigerator.

COAL-ROASTED PEPPERS

Gardening (or farming) and cooking are the two most basic, yet most direct connections we have with the land. Very few humans still hunt as their sole means of supplying their families with food, although recreational hunters generally eat what they bag. Cooking over an open fire is an age-old technology that was developed when man began to hunt. This leads me to my point that cooking over fire is a sure way to connect with our past—and food cooked this way tastes so good! I like to think that we love the flavor of open-fired food because we've been enjoying the method for millennia. When you combine gardening with this primal cooking style, just our olfactory sensations alone evoke feelings of warmth and security that are inexplicable. Add our other sensations and you have a winner! Coal-roasted peppers bring the garden and the grill together.

Most of us are familiar with roasting peppers, either over an open flame or in an oven. We marvel at how the charred skin makes the peppers look ruined and burned beyond redemption, but then, of course, the skins slip easily off the peppers to reveal a moist, lushly colored, and densely flavored flesh that is a favorite ingredient in many cultures.

Coal roasting the peppers is another method that achieves similar results. I get a kick out of how simple this is and how easily it freaks out my friends. Here's how to do it: Begin with freshly picked hot or sweet peppers, wash and dry the skins, and then bury them in the hot coals of a charcoal grill. You can do this while you're grilling other foods. Leave them buried until the skins blacken, which will take 5 to 10 minutes, and then transfer them to a covered bowl to steam.

After 15 minutes or so, when the peppers are cool enough to handle, rub off the skins, taking care not to rub too hard; you don't have to get rid of every little bit of charred skin. Rinse them quickly under cool running water to rid them of any ash and then cut them open. The flavor is amazing!

If you want to roast a batch of sweet bell peppers to keep in the refrigerator for salads, soups, sauces, and antipasti, you can store them in extra-virgin olive oil along with your favorite herb. Here's how: When you are done grilling a meal, remove the grate from the grill. Use a large metal spatula or small shovel to push most of the hot coals to one side, but leave a thin layer of coals over most of the floor of the grill. Lay as many whole peppers as you can fit comfortably on top of the thin layer of coals. Pile the rest of the hot ashes and coals over the peppers to cover completely. Wait for about 5 minutes, or until the skins are well blackened. Proceed as above.

To store these peppers, after you slice them, layer them with herbs in glass or rigid plastic containers with tight-fitting lids and refrigerate for up to 1 week. You can also cover the peppers with olive oil and refrigerate them for up to 3 weeks.

Rosemary-Orange SALT

MAKES
ABOUT 1¼ CUPS

EVERY KITCHEN SHOULD BE EQUIPPED WITH A GOOD MORTAR AND PESTLE, the best tools ever developed for crushing herbs, spices, and seeds. The mortar is the bowl, which may be of varying sizes and made of marble, stone, or wood or of porcelain with a textured, abrasive surface. The blunt pestle usually is made from the same material as the bowl, although it may be made of hardwood as well. While you can grind, purée, or blend foods in a spice grinder or food processor, you have better control with a mortar and pestle, especially with small amounts. Making this salt is a good example of how this age-old tool comes in handy!

I CUP COARSE SEA SALT
such as fleur de sel

**2 TABLESPOONS
FRESH ROSEMARY LEAVES**

**I TEASPOON BLACK
PEPPERCORNS**

**I TEASPOON FRESH FENNEL
SEEDS** (from flower head at full seed)

ZEST OF 6 ORANGES,
cut into julienne

I. In a sauté pan, combine the salt, rosemary, peppercorns, and fennel seeds over medium-high heat and cook, shaking the pan gently, for 2 to 3 minutes, or until the pan gets hot and the salt and fennel seeds begin to crackle.

2. Remove the pan from the heat, add the orange zest, and toss with the salt for about 2 minutes, or until the pan begins to cool.

3. Spread the salt over a dry baking sheet and set aside to cool completely.

4. Transfer small batches of the salt mixture to a mortar. Using a pestle, crush to the consistency you prefer. I like mine a little coarse. Alternatively, grind the salt mixture in a spice grinder or a coffee grinder reserved for spices.

5. Store the salt in an airtight container in a cool, dry place for up to 4 months.

Michel's
SPICE POWDER

MAKES
ABOUT ¼ CUP

USE THIS ON BEEF, PORK, LAMB, OR CHICKEN, OR ADD IT TO SAUCES AND DRESSINGS. I like to use soft *canela,* sometimes called Mexican cinnamon, for its mellowness, but any cinnamon will work.

2 TABLESPOONS CORIANDER SEEDS

1 TABLESPOON CUMIN SEEDS

2 TEASPOONS MUSTARD SEEDS

1 GREEN CARDAMOM POD
or ¼ teaspoon ground cardamom

½-INCH-LONG PIECE CANELA (Mexican cinnamon)
or 1 teaspoon ground cinnamon

1. In a small sauté pan, combine the coriander seeds, cumin seeds, mustard seeds, cardamom pod, and cinnamon. (If using ground cardamom or ground cinnamon, add later.) Place over medium heat and heat, shaking the pan gently and constantly, for about 1 minute, or until fragrant.

2. Remove from the heat and add the ground cardamom or ground cinnamon, if using. Stir to mix. Pour onto a large, flat plate or baking sheet to cool.

3. Remove the cardamom pod (if using) and chop it with a sturdy knife.

4. Transfer the chopped cardamom and the rest of the cooled spices to a spice grinder or a coffee grinder reserved for spices. Pulse until the mixture resembles coarse cornmeal.

5. Store in an airtight container at room temperature for up to 2 weeks.

A COUPLE OF DRINKS

WHILE DRINKS MAY NOT FIT PERFECTLY IN A CHAPTER ABOUT EXTENDING THE HARVEST, they provide a delightful and unexpected way to get the most from your garden. For this reason, you might think of herb- and flower-infused drinks as "harvest expanders." Both iced tea and lemonade are great thirst quenchers for any hardworking gardener, and here I show you how to make one of each by going beyond the usual boundaries.

When I brew iced or hot, tea, I use loose tea leaves. Tea bags, even the more expensive ones, often are nothing more than the sweepings or the lowliest scraps of the tea plant. Well-packaged loose teas have flavor qualities that will surprise and please you, and brewing it is not as much of a hassle as you may think. I like to buy premium loose tea leaves from teahouses and coffee bars. One of my favorite sources is Ten Ren Tea Company (see Sources, page 221), specializing in black, oolong, white, and green teas from China and other places in the Far East, but there are others. Do your own investigation. It's fun.

For the iced tea here, I turn to my all-time favorite tea, Darjeeling from Darjeeling, India. This is considered by many connoisseurs to be the finest tea grown. Certainly it is the standard by which I judge most other teas, and I always come back to it. I let the seductive flavor blending of peach and cinnamon play off the nuttiness of the tea and then, to make this chilled beverage sing, add a sprig of something green.

You can use mint, but go beyond it and try basil, lemon verbena, lemon thyme, tarragon, or pineapple sage. All of these herbs bring significant aromatic qualities, freshness, and beauty to a tall glass of iced tea—and you can cut them from the garden to fit the glass.

My recipe for lemonade takes issue with the theory that lemonade must be made with lemon juice and water. Try watermelon juice instead. The watermelon may be made mostly of water, but its luscious sweetness and mesmerizing color combine with lemon juice to make an outstanding summer refresher. This is a good use for those mint sprigs happily growing in the garden, too.

WATERMELON LEMONADE

SERVES
4

I SMALL WATERMELON
(about 6 pounds)

6 LEMONS

¼ CUP LOCAL HONEY

4 LARGE FRESH MINT SPRIGS

I. To peel the watermelon, slice off both ends just to the flesh so that the watermelon will stand upright on a cutting board. Using a large knife, slice the rind from the flesh, working from the top to the bottom in one long stroke if possible. Repeat, using the white of the rind as a guide for the knife, until the melon is completely peeled.

2. Cut the melon into large cubes and juice in a heavy-duty juicer. Alternatively, put the cubes in a very large bowl, get your kids or a friend, wash your hands, and smash the living daylights out of the melon flesh. Pour the mash through a fine-mesh sieve placed over a bowl. You should have about 4 cups juice.

3. Using your palm, roll each lemon forcefully on a work surface. This breaks the membranes under the skin and frees the juice. Cut the lemons in half and squeeze the juice through a fine sieve into a small nonreactive saucepan.

4. Add the honey to the lemon juice and warm over low heat just until the honey liquefies. Add the lemon-honey mixture to the watermelon juice.

5. Rub the mint sprigs vigorously between your palms to release their oils and then add them to the lemonade. Cover and refrigerate for 2 hours, or until well chilled, before serving.

Peach and Cinnamon
DARJEELING TEA

MAKES ABOUT 5 QUARTS

6 CINNAMON STICKS

4 QUARTS HOT, BREWED DARJEELING TEA

8 VERY RIPE PEACHES

6 FRESH LEMON VERBENA SPRIGS or basil sprigs

I. Holding the cinnamon sticks with tongs, toast them an inch or so above a high gas flame for about 1 minute, or until they darken a shade and are fragrant. You can also set them directly on a hot electric coil and turn them as they toast. This takes 20 to 30 seconds. With either method, be sure to wear oven mitts or use a reliable pot holder. Set aside.

2. Add the toasted cinnamon sticks to the hot tea. Set the tea aside to cool to room temperature.

3. Meanwhile, using a sharp paring knife, peel 2 of the peaches, and then halve and pit them. Pulse in a mini processor or a blender until smooth. Add the peach purée to the tea as it cools.

4. Peel the 6 remaining peaches, cut them into quarters, and add them to the tea while it is still warm, but not hot.

5. When the tea is at room temperature, add the lemon verbena. Cover and refrigerate for 2 hours, or until well chilled, before serving.

NOTE: This recipe can easily be halved.

JUICING FRUITS AND VEGETABLES

WHEN YOU JUICE FRUITS AND VEGETABLES, BUY MORE THAN YOU THINK YOU WILL NEED. The yield varies depending on the moisture content of the particular item, when and where it was harvested, and how it was stored. If you get more juice than you need, don't worry about it. Drink any juice you don't use or pour it into another preparation. I particularly like carrot juice, and all fruit juices, and most vegetable juices, although I suspect potato or summer squash juice wouldn't be too tasty as drinks. Freshly made juices don't keep well, so use them promptly. The exceptions are those that are naturally acidic, such as citrus juices and apple juice. They will keep in the refrigerator for about a day.

To prepare fruits and vegetables for juicing, wash them under cool running water and cut away any soft spots. Scrub root vegetables lightly with a coarse pad or brush, but there is no need to peel them. Slice or cut fruits and vegetables into manageable sizes. Remove large pits and seeds, but there is no need to scrape out all seeds or remove stems. Any good heavy-duty juicer will take care of them.

When you are done juicing, you will be left with pulp. You can use this in some dishes and baked goods, as I have in SWEET POTATO BREAKFAST BREAD (page 193), or toss it on the compost pile. The compost is a vital component to any garden and pulp from the juicer is a welcome addition.

FOR I CUP JUICE (amounts are approximate)

APPLES: **1 pound**

ASPARAGUS: **1 pound**

BEETS: **1 pound**

CARROTS: **1 pound**

CELERY: **1 pound**

CHERRIES: **1 pound**

CORN KERNELS: **1 pound**
(about 3 cups; from 6 or 7 ears)

ENGLISH PEAS: **1 pound** (I cup shelled)

FENNEL: **12 ounces**

GOLDEN BEETS: **12 ounces**

PEARS: **1 pound**

PLUMS: **1 pound**

RUTABAGAS: **12 ounces**

SUMMER SQUASHES: **1¼ pounds**

SWEET POTATOES: **1¼ pounds**

YUKON GOLD POTATOES: **1¼ pounds**

WATERMELON: **1 to 1½ pounds**

ROASTING VEGETABLES

ROASTING VEGETABLES ACCENTUATES
THEIR NATURAL FLAVORS AND SWEETNESS
and is one of the best ways to serve them—not to
mention one of the easiest. Roasting times vary
depending on the moisture and starch content of the
vegetable. These two elements are dependent on the
season the vegetable was cultivated, the rainfall during
germination and growth, and the way the vegetable
was stored after harvest. All these factors make roasting an inexact science.

To prepare vegetables for roasting, wash them
under cool running water. Scrub root vegetables with
a coarse pad or brush, rather than peel them. So many
nutrients exist in the skin, it's a shame to strip them
away. Scrubbing tenderizes the skin and removes any
root hairs, which could burn during roasting.

Rub the vegetables with water or grapeseed oil
and season with salt and freshly ground black pepper,
unless a recipe specifies a different treatment. Lay
them on a baking sheet and roast in a preheated 300°F
(unless otherwise instructed) until tender.

APPROXIMATE ROASTING TIMES

BEETS:
20 TO 30 MINUTES FOR BABY BEETS
45 TO 60 MINUTES FOR MEDIUM BEETS

CARROTS:
15 TO 20 MINUTES FOR BABY CARROTS
30 TO 40 MINUTES FOR MEDIUM CARROTS

ONIONS:
30 TO 40 MINUTES

PARSNIPS:
PARBOIL IN SIMMERING WATER FOR 15 MINUTES
THEN ROAST FOR 15 TO 20 MINUTES

PEARL OR CIPOLLINI ONIONS:
15 TO 20 MINUTES

POTATOES (white, purple, Yukon Gold):
15 TO 20 MINUTES FOR WEDGES

RADISHES:
15 MINUTES FOR SMALL RADISHES
25 MINUTES FOR LARGE RADISHES

SCALLIONS:
15 TO 20 MINUTES

SHALLOTS:
10 TO 15 MINUTES

SUMMER SQUASHES:
20 TO 25 MINUTES FOR WEDGES
10 TO 15 MINUTES FOR 1-INCH CUBES

SWEET POTATOES:
15 MINUTES FOR WEDGES

TURNIPS:
8 TO 12 MINUTES FOR BABY TURNIPS
15 TO 25 MINUTES FOR MEDIUM TURNIPS

WINTER SQUASHES:
35 TO 40 MINUTES FOR WEDGES
25 TO 30 MINUTES FOR 1-INCH CUBES

breakfast
and breads

MY FIRST RESTAURANT JOB WAS AS A BREAKFAST COOK AT CENTER'S TRUCK STOP NEAR ANTIOCH, ILLINOIS, and to this day, I can cook eggs any which way with my arms tied behind my back! Back then, the highway ran through cornfields and I loved watching the morning light over the fields as I worked. So for me, morning and food are closely associated. I consider starting the day right with the "most important meal" to be more than a cliché. It's reality.

In the spring, summer, and fall, I get up early to work in the garden whenever I can. As I cultivate, plant, weed, or harvest and start to get hungry, I think about how I can work some of the vegetables and herbs flourishing around me into breakfast, or how fantastic a batch of muffins would smell baking in the oven. Morning also makes me think of picking berries or gathering eggs. All this inspires me to celebrate the bounties of the garden in one of my favorite meals. While many folks don't think of breakfast as a garden-friendly meal, I aim to change that with the following recipes.

Maple and Black Raspberry
PANCAKES

SERVES
3

DOES MAPLE SYRUP HAVE A SEASON? You bet your bottom dollar it does! In fact, Native Americans once celebrated the early spring awakening of the maple trees. As soon as the days showed a little warmth, the trees offered their lifeblood, or sap, and the native peoples rejoiced by enjoying the rewarding sweetness and nutrients flowing through the noble trees. They shared this wonder with the early settlers, who then waited patiently for the end of winter to replenish the syrup stocks that had run out. Interestingly, maple syrup was once the only affordable sweetener around, which explains why so many eighteenth-century American recipes relied on it. When Caribbean trade made cane sugar readily available, maple syrup was relegated to dressing griddle cakes and corn mush.

This recipe breaks maple syrup out of the box! Most of us think only of pouring it straight from the bottle over pancakes or waffles, but I use it to sweeten the pancake batter and also mix it with fresh orange juice and berries for a thick, chunky syrup. I love the syrup in this recipe over pancakes and waffles, but I also use it to glaze chicken and pork.

Black raspberries, one of my favorite berries, grow easily in most gardens and hedgerows. In fact, once the raspberry bushes are established, you have to prune them every year to keep them from taking over! When you mix the berries with orange juice and maple syrup, their flavor perks up with a sweet tang, and the natural nutrients in the berries and juice are beneficial for everyone. While I call for black raspberries, you can make this with red or golden raspberries or any mixture of the three.

continued

maple and black raspberry pancakes

continued

MAPLE–BLACK RASPBERRY SYRUP

1 CUP FRESH ORANGE JUICE

1 CINNAMON STICK

2 TABLESPOONS GRATED ORANGE ZEST

1 CUP REAL MAPLE SYRUP

⅔ CUP BLACK RASPBERRIES or red or golden raspberries, or a mixture

PANCAKES

2 TO 3 ORANGES

1 CUP UNBLEACHED ALL-PURPOSE FLOUR

2 TEASPOONS BAKING POWDER

¼ TEASPOON SALT

½ CUP WHOLE OR 2-PERCENT MILK

1 LARGE EGG, well beaten

2 TEASPOONS GRAPESEED OIL

¾ CUP BLACK RASPBERRIES or red or golden raspberries, or a mixture

1. To make the syrup, combine the orange juice and cinnamon stick in a small saucepan over medium heat and simmer for 7 to 8 minutes, or until reduced to ½ cup.

2. Add the orange zest and maple syrup and stir to mix. Add the berries and mash gently with a fork to release the flavors and juices. Strain the syrup through a fine-mesh sieve. Cover and set aside to keep warm while you make the pancakes. You should have about 1½ cups syrup.

3. To make the pancakes, grate the zest of 2 of the oranges. (I like to use a Microplane grater.) Be careful not to grate the white pith that is beneath the colored part of the peel. Set the zest aside.

4. Cut the oranges in half and squeeze out the juice. You will need ½ cup. If necessary, squeeze the third orange to measure the full ½ cup.

5. In a bowl, whisk together the flour, baking powder, and salt. Add the orange zest, milk, orange juice, and egg. Stir the batter just until combined but still lumpy. (If you overbeat the batter so that it's smooth, the pancakes will be tough.)

6. Heat a nonstick skillet or griddle over medium-high heat. When hot, lightly oil the pan by moistening a clean kitchen towel with the oil and rubbing it over the bottom of the pan. Working in batches if necessary, ladle the batter into the pan, using a generous ¼ cup for each pancake and spacing the pancakes about 1 inch apart. Scatter a few berries over each pancake; they will sink into the batter. Cook for about 1 minute, or until the tops of the pancakes bubble. Turn and cook for about 30 seconds longer, gently pushing on the pancakes to cook the berries. You will have 6 plump pancakes, each 4 to 5 inches in diameter.

7. Serve the pancakes immediately and pass the warm syrup at the table.

Ranchero-Style STEAK and EGGS

SERVES 6

WHEN I FIRST MOVED TO MILWAUKEE, WISCONSIN, I LIVED ACROSS FROM A WONDERFUL LITTLE MEXICAN RESTAURANT CALLED LA CASITA. All I had to do to enjoy their weekend brunch was to roll out of bed and walk across the street. One of my favorite dishes was huevos rancheros, or "ranchers' eggs," a lively dish that was especially good with ice-cold Mexican beer.

The cooks at La Casita sautéed onions, bell peppers, garlic, and spicy sausage in a skillet and then cracked in a couple of sunny-side-up eggs. The only down side to this mouthwatering dish was the moisture from the peppers and onions that collected at the bottom of the pan, which didn't mix with the egg whites.

My recipe eliminates this watery quality by scrambling some of the eggs. I also use trimmings from the RIB-EYE STEAKS WITH SAVORY HERBS AND ROASTED GARLIC. These trimmings are delicious, of course, but you should think of this recipe as a creative way to use other leftovers, too, such as any cubed leftover steak, pork roast, or pot roast; your favorite turkey, chicken, or pork sausage; or even salmon with a little fresh dill added to the pan. The rule is that anything goes, as long as the ingredients taste good together.

To ensure that the eggs cook evenly, I want to share two tricks. First, keep the eggs you will scramble chilled until right before cooking them. Whisk them lightly with a fork in a bowl and refrigerate them. This prevents them from cooking quickly. Second, the whole eggs should be tempered, or warmed up slightly, and cracked into a shallow bowl. This way, you don't have to fuss with cracking them when the heat is on (pun intended). The scrambled eggs are cooked before the whole eggs are added to the pan, so planning is critical.

6 OUNCES LEFTOVER BEEF FROM RIB-EYE STEAKS WITH SAVORY HERBS AND ROASTED GARLIC (page 83) or other steak leftovers, cut into I-inch cubes

SALT AND FRESHLY GROUND BLACK PEPPER

2 TABLESPOONS GRAPESEED OR RICE OIL

¼ CUP SLICED YELLOW ONION

I CUP ½-INCH-DICE ZUCCHINI, YELLOW, OR PATTYPAN SQUASH

I SERRANO OR LARGE JALAPEÑO CHILI, seeded and diced

2 THIN SLICES HABANERO CHILI

5 LARGE EGGS, well beaten and kept cold

I ROASTED RED BELL PEPPER, seeded and cut lengthwise into ½-inch-wide strips (see Note, page 25)

I ROASTED YELLOW BELL PEPPER, seeded and cut lengthwise into ½-inch-wide strips (see Note, page 25)

I½ TEASPOONS FRESH THYME LEAVES

6 LARGE EGGS IN THE SHELL, tempered in hot water, cracked into a bowl, and kept at room temperature (see Note)

GRAPESEED OR RICE OIL in a mister or spray bottle

¼ CUP COARSELY GRATED AGED CHEDDAR CHEESE

I TABLESPOON SLICED FRESH CHIVES

1. Preheat the broiler and position the broiler rack about 6 inches from the heating element.

2. Season the steak with salt and pepper and set aside.

3. Heat a 12-inch cast-iron skillet over medium heat. When hot, add the oil, immediately followed by the steak and onion. Sauté, stirring occasionally, for 2 to 2½ minutes, or until the meat is browned on all sides and the onion is translucent. Using a slotted spoon or spatula, remove the steak and reserve.

4. Add the squash and the serrano and habanero chilies to the onion remaining in the pan and sauté, stirring occasionally, for 4 to 5 minutes, or until the squash begins to soften and the onion browns.

5. Add the 5 beaten eggs, roasted peppers, thyme, and reserved steak. Stir with a wooden spatula for 3 to 4 minutes, or until the eggs turn into a soft, wet scramble. Remove the pan from the heat and make a well in the center of the scrambled egg mixture. Slide the whole eggs into the well and use the wooden spatula to manipulate the egg yolks so that they are evenly arranged in the center of the well. Stir the edges of the egg whites into the surrounding scrambled eggs.

6. Mist the exposed egg yolks lightly with oil, sprinkle with the Cheddar cheese, and transfer the pan to the broiler. Broil for about 1 minute, or until the cheese just begins to melt and the yolks look cooked.

7. Remove from the broiler and sprinkle with the chives. Carry the skillet to the table and let the hungry rancheros fend for themselves.

NOTE: To temper the eggs, submerge them in very hot tap water for about 2 minutes, or leave them on the kitchen counter for 20 to 30 minutes to bring them to room temperature. Crack them into a shallow bowl (a cereal bowl will do), taking care they don't break. You will be able to slide them whole into the skillet with ease.

GARDEN VEGETABLE FRITTATA

**SERVES
8 TO 10**

WE ARE EAGER TO TRY RAISING CHICKENS ON OUR SUBURBAN PROPERTY FOR FOUR REASONS. First, we need the manure to heat and decompose our compost pile properly. Second, we've heard intriguing stories about chickens that taste amazing when fed select table scraps, such as roasted garlic. Third, I am pretty sure the chickens will do a better job than I can of picking potato beetles off my eggplants. Fourth, breakfast never tasted better than what my mom made with fresh eggs and vegetables from my grandpa's farm.

Farm fresh eggs are recognizably richer in color, taste, and texture than eggs that have been pasteurized and stored for weeks for grocery-store distribution. Many of my readers are well aware of the notable difference between a store-bought and a homegrown tomato. The difference between a farm-fresh egg and a supermarket egg is just as dramatic.

You may not be as crazy as we are and try to raise chickens in your backyard, but you can look for a local farmers' market where chicken farmers sell eggs. During the last twenty-five years, I have lived in a dozen cities in four different areas of the country and have always been able to find farm-fresh eggs. If you're having trouble, go on the Web and Google your state's department of agriculture. Look for links to farmers' markets, farm co-op stores, and local IGAs (stores run by the Independent Grocer's Association) that feature in-state farm-fresh products. You may be as hopeless on the computer as I am, and so you can always check the information pages of the telephone book for much of the same information. Truly fresh eggs are often a phone call and leisurely Saturday drive away.

2 TO 3 TABLESPOONS OLIVE OIL

I TABLESPOON UNSALTED BUTTER

2 SMALL YUKON GOLD OR PURPLE POTATOES, peeled, if desired, and thinly sliced (about ¾ cup)

I EGGPLANT (about I pound), peeled and cut into I-inch cubes

SALT AND FRESHLY GROUND BLACK PEPPER

2 LARGE, VERY RIPE TOMATOES, cored, seeded, and cut into large chunks

8 SCALLIONS, white and green parts, sliced (about I cup)

I2 LARGE EGGS

½ CUP WHOLE OR 2-PERCENT MILK

½ CUP HEAVY CREAM

½ CUP CHOPPED MIXED FRESH HERBS such as basil, chives, dill, flat-leaf parsley, and lavender

¾ CUP GRATED SHARP CHEDDAR CHEESE

½ CUP CRUMBLED FRESH GOAT CHEESE

I. Preheat the oven to 350°F.

2. Heat a well-seasoned 12-inch cast-iron skillet over medium heat. Add the oil and butter and heat until the butter sizzles. Add the potatoes, spread in a single layer, and cook on one side for 2 to 3 minutes, or until nicely browned. Using a spatula, turn over the potatoes and move to side of pan.

3. Meanwhile, season the eggplant with salt and pepper. When you turn the potatoes, add the eggplant to the skillet and cook for 3 to 4 minutes, or until the eggplant cubes are browned on at least 2 sides. Add more oil, if necessary. By this time, the potatoes should be browned on both sides, too.

4. Add the tomato chunks and cook for about 3 minutes, or until any liquid they release has nearly evaporated. Push to the side of the pan and add the scallions and cook for about 30 seconds, or until slightly softened. Distribute the vegetables evenly in the pan with a wooden spoon or spatula.

5. In a large bowl, whisk together the eggs, milk, cream, herbs, and half of the grated Cheddar cheese. Season with salt and pepper.

6. Slowly pour the eggs into the skillet, being careful not to dislodge the vegetables. Reduce the heat to low and cook for 6 to 8 minutes without stirring, or until the frittata is partially set.

7. Sprinkle the goat cheese evenly over the top and transfer to the oven. Bake the frittata for about 20 minutes, or until nearly set but not yet browned on top. Sprinkle with the remaining Cheddar cheese and return to the oven for about 5 minutes, or until the cheese is melted and browned.

8. Serve the frittata directly from the skillet, cut into wedges.

BREAD

WHILE I DON'T HAVE MANY BREAD RECIPES IN THIS BOOK, I URGE YOU NEVER TO STOP BAKING BREAD. It's one of the more rewarding kitchen tasks and the results are stupendous, particularly if you stay away from overprocessed white flour and focus on whole-wheat flour and specialty grains that add flavor, such as rye, buckwheat, rice, oats, spelt, amaranth, and semolina. You don't have to make your own bread to benefit from it. Bakeries from coast to coast produce outstanding artisanal loaves, made from whole, healthful grains. These bakers care about what they sell and yet they are going out of business in record numbers lately because bread is facing a crisis, promulgated by the ill-advised and narrowly informed low-carb craze. It's time to fight back and address this gimmicky approach head on.

Since the distant days of early agriculture, bread has been the so-called staff of life, sustaining generations all around the globe, and yet in a short few years we have turned the familiar loaf into a villain. In our frenzy to oversimplify health issues, we decided that carbohydrates are "bad" and promptly turned our backs on an entire food group. What we should turn our backs on are the monster carbs produced by modern food science in its never-ending quest to bring the public the convenience and the low-cost "garbage foods" (my words) too many people have come to rely on. I am all for low costs, of course, but there are times when health is more important. Frankly, bread and flour are never going to be high-ticket items in the family budget, and so it makes good sense to buy bread and other foods made from whole grains and feed your family right.

There is no denying the significant short-term benefits of a low-carb diet, but it is equally apparent that longer-term dangers loom. Many of the people who turn to the quick fix of a low-carb diet are leaving a regimen that includes gorging on fast, snack, and convenience foods. These contain all the "bad carbs," such as white sugar, white flour, and high-fructose corn syrup, the very things that got these desperate dieters into trouble in the first place. These "empty foods" also contain lethal trans fats, which are common partners to toxic "bad carbs." It stands to reason that the kind of carbohydrates you eat go a long way toward helping you lose weight. I truly believe you should not rob yourself or your family of the wonderful flavors and significant health benefits of artisanal breads.

Your kids may be hooked on white bread and, as the father of five kids, I know it can be a huge hassle to break them of the habit. Teaching our children about healthful eating and good carbohydrates is one of the greatest favors we can do for them. Read the labels when you shop. Instead of vilifying carbs, we only have to learn about wholesome "good carbs" and start enjoying one of life's small and consistent pleasures again: freshly baked bread.

Sweet Potato
BREAKFAST BREAD

**MAKES 1 LOAF;
SERVES 10 TO 12**

I MAY CALL THIS A BREAKFAST BREAD, BUT IT'S GOOD ALL DAY LONG. It is a delicious way to use sweet potato pulp left from juicing, and because it is made with spelt flour, it is a recipe designed for those with sensitivities to wheat. In my book *Taste: Pure and Simple,* I neglected to provide recipes for the pulp left in the juicer and am rectifying that oversight with this recipe. Take my lead and use other vegetable pulps, such as white potato and winter squash, in your own quick-bread and muffin recipes.

Spelt is an ancient grain from the same family as oats and wheat but a different species with more health benefits. It was first cultivated at least nine thousand years ago, in the Fertile Crescent, today's Iraq, along with other grains. Italians call a similar grain *farro,* while Germans call it *dinkel.* Its nutrients, which include protein, riboflavin, niacin, iron, and potassium, are easily absorbed by the body and are great immune boosters. It's packed with B-complex vitamins and is a terrific source of fiber. While spelt contains some gluten, it's generally well tolerated by anyone who has trouble digesting wheat.

continued

FLAVORLESS VEGETABLE OIL
SPRAY AND SPELT FLOUR for
preparing pan

2 CINNAMON STICKS

I CUP FRESHLY PRESSED
APPLE JUICE or apple cider,
plus more if needed

I STAR ANISE POD

I CUP SWEET POTATO PULP
(from I½ pounds sweet potatoes)

¼ TEASPOON FRESHLY GRATED
NUTMEG

I½ CUPS SPELT FLOUR

I¼ TEASPOONS BAKING SODA

I TEASPOON SALT

½ CUP LOCAL HONEY

¼ CUP ORGANIC PLAIN
WHOLE-MILK YOGURT

¼ CUP SOFT FRESH GOAT CHEESE

I LARGE EGG

2 TABLESPOONS OLIVE OIL

1. Preheat the oven to 350°F. Lightly spray a 9-by-5-inch loaf pan with vegetable oil spray. Dust it lightly with spelt flour.

2. Holding the cinnamon sticks with tongs, toast them an inch or so above a high gas flame for about 1 minute, or until they darken a shade and are fragrant. You can also set them directly on a hot electric coil and turn them as they toast. This takes 20 to 30 seconds. With either method, be sure to wear oven mitts or use a reliable pot holder.

3. In a saucepan, mix together the apple juice, star anise, and cinnamon sticks over medium heat and simmer gently for about 10 minutes to infuse the apple juice with the spices. Remove from the heat and let sit for 15 minutes. Discard the cinnamon sticks and star anise.

4. Add the sweet potato pulp and nutmeg to the pan and cook over low heat for 8 to 10 minutes, or until the mixture forms a smooth paste. Add a little more apple juice if the pulp seems dry.

5. In a bowl, sift together the flour, baking soda, and salt and whisk to ensure thorough mixing. Slowly stir in the sweet potato pulp mixture.

6. In a small bowl, whisk together the honey, yogurt, goat cheese, and egg. Add the oil and whisk again until smooth. Fold in the sweet potato mixture.

7. Pour the batter into the prepared pan and bake for 60 to 70 minutes, or until a toothpick inserted into the center comes out clean.

8. Let the bread cool in the pan on a wire rack for about 5 minutes. Turn the loaf out of the pan and let cool completely on the rack.

Butternut Squash
MUFFINS

MAKES
12
MUFFINS

IF YOU HAVEN'T THOUGHT OF BUTTERNUT SQUASH FOR MUFFINS BEFORE, here's a good opportunity to try it. Like such vegetables as zucchini and carrots, the squash adds moisture, texture, and pleasing flavor along with a host of vitamins and other nutrients. See the introduction to SWEET POTATO BREAKFAST BREAD (PAGE 193) for information on spelt flour, another healthful addition to this muffin batter.

FLAVORLESS VEGETABLE OIL SPRAY or grapeseed or rice oil in a mister or spray bottle (optional)

I POUND BUTTERNUT SQUASH, peeled, seeded, and cut into small cubes (about 3 cups)

I TEASPOON COARSE SEA SALT

8 BLACK PEPPERCORNS

2 CINNAMON STICKS

2 TABLESPOONS CORIANDER SEEDS

4 CUPS FRESHLY PRESSED APPLE JUICE or apple cider

I CUP RAW CANE SUGAR

2 LARGE EGG YOLKS

½ CUP HOMEMADE APPLESAUCE (page 166)

¼ CUP GRAPESEED OR RICE OIL

4 LARGE EGG WHITES

I. Preheat the oven to 350°F. Spray a 12-cup muffin tin with the oil, or put paper liners in the cups. Spray a rimmed baking sheet as well, or line with parchment paper.

2. Toss the squash with the coarse sea salt and spread in a single layer on the prepared baking sheet. Bake for 20 to 30 minutes, or until the squash is cooked through and tender.

3. Meanwhile, in a saucepan, combine the peppercorns, cinnamon sticks, and coriander over medium-high heat and heat for 2 to 3 minutes, or until the coriander begins to smell like oranges. Remove from the heat, let sit for 30 seconds, and then add the apple juice. Return to the heat and simmer for 30 to 40 minutes, or until reduced to ¼ cup and thick. Pour the apple juice through a fine-mesh sieve, discard the whole spices and push the reduced juice through the sieve with the back of a spoon, if necessary. Set aside.

4. Transfer the squash and reduced juice to a food processor and process until smooth.

5. In the bowl of an electric mixer fitted with the paddle attachment, beat together the sugar and egg yolks on high speed for about 3 minutes, or until light and fluffy. Reduce the speed to low and mix in the applesauce, oil, and butternut squash purée just until blended. Transfer to a large bowl.

2 CUPS SPELT FLOUR

2¼ TEASPOON BAKING POWDER

I TEASPOON BAKING SODA

I TEASPOON FINE SEA SALT

6. Fit the mixer with the whip attachment and clean and dry the bowl. Add the egg whites to the bowl and beat on medium-high speed until very foamy, but not quite soft peaks.

7. In another bowl, whisk together the flour, baking powder, baking soda, and the fine sea salt. Add to the batter and stir just until mixed. Then fold in the egg whites just until blended. There will be some white streaks in the batter, which is fine.

8. Spoon the batter into the muffin cups, filling each one about three-fourths full. Bake for 30 to 40 minutes, or until a toothpick inserted into the center of a muffin comes out clean.

9. Let the muffins cool in the tin on a wire rack for about 5 minutes. Turn the muffins out of the tin and let cool completely on the rack before serving.

CHAPTER

8

desserts

I HAVE NEVER BEEN ESPECIALLY INTERESTED IN DESSERT, WHICH IS UNDOUBTEDLY BECAUSE I GREW UP WITH A JUICY, RIPE PEACH IN ONE HAND AND PLUMP, SWEET BERRIES IN THE OTHER. When you've tasted local honey drizzled over an apple you've just picked from the orchard, you can't imagine mucking it up with flour, sugar, and butter (although I admit that a good apple pie is pretty darned tasty!).

An exception to my affinity for more natural sweets is my mother's angel food cake. Making it is a way for me to reach out and touch her hand. Over the years, I have added some of my own touches to her recipe, but it is true to her original sweet intent. I use almond flour rather than almond extract, which makes the cake a little denser, but I like it that way.

I also have included a recipe that speaks to the brilliance of my mother's frugality. Angel food cake is delicious eaten on the day it's baked, but after that, its allure diminishes by the hour. Mom solved this by slicing it and frying it in butter and then drizzling the toasted cake with honey. I may be known for cooking for health and well-being, but I also say it ain't bad to be sinful every now and then. If you're going to stray, stray with this!

The other desserts in this chapter are celebrations of fruit, nuts, and even fresh sweet corn, reminders that for every overly sweet, gloppy dessert there are dozens of juicy, ripe fruits for the picking and immediate enjoyment.

Roasted PEAR and SPOON BREAD TART
with Cranberry, Orange, and Jalapeño Glaze

**SERVES
8**

THIS IS A GREAT FALL DESSERT THAT MAKES THE MOST OF THE RIPE, LUSCIOUS PEARS, such as Bosc or Anjou, that are in supermarkets, farmers' markets, and, if you're lucky, your own backyard. Because they are not cooked for long, the pears you select must be perfectly ripe. Choose fragrant, smooth fruits with their stems still attached. Don't worry about blemishes as much as ripeness. Pears that are picked ripe might not be picture-perfect, but their flavor, texture, and nutrient load is so far superior to the standard supermarket fare (picked and shipped weeks before they ripen), comparisons are almost irrelevant. Ripe pears will feel heavy and slightly soft. This softness should extend all the way to the area around the stem. If you are working with underripe pears, let them sit at room temperature until they soften a little more. Avoid any that are hard and unforgiving. Cooking

pears too long alters their flavor and causes them to taste "processed," like canned pears. Treat them as I do here for fresh flavor.

Since it is made with spoon bread, a savory quick bread, this is not a typical tart. I use spoon bread because it tastes so good with the pears and the spicy-sweet, slightly chunky glaze, and also because cornmeal is a good carbohydrate. Stone-ground organic yellow cornmeal is packed with healthful minerals and other nutrients, and when you buy it in the fall, chances are it was recently ground. Make sure you buy the real thing for this recipe. Small mills, such as Anson Mills, grind it for sale (for more on this company, see Sources on page 221). If you can find cornmeal ground from Iroquois white corn, try it. The small-batch flours taste fresh, pure, and almost nutty. I use yellow cornmeal for this recipe mainly because my mom used it, but you can use another.

continued

roasted pear and spoon bread tart
with cranberry, orange, and jalapeño glaze

continued

I CUP WATER

I CUP STONE-GROUND YELLOW CORNMEAL (see Note)

I TABLESPOON UNSALTED BUTTER, at room temperature

I TABLESPOON GRAPESEED OIL

I TABLESPOON LOCAL HONEY

I TEASPOON FINE SEA SALT

I CUP NONFAT MILK

I LARGE WHOLE EGG PLUS 2 LARGE EGG WHITES, beaten until well blended

FLAVORLESS VEGETABLE OIL SPRAY

3 NICELY RIPENED PEARS (about 12 ounces total), peeled, halved, cored, and thinly sliced

½ TEASPOON GROUND CINNAMON

¼ TO ½ CUP CRANBERRY, ORANGE, AND JALAPEÑO GLAZE (page 204), warmed

1. Preheat the oven to 375°F.

2. Bring the water to a boil in a saucepan. Remove the pan from the heat and, stirring constantly, slowly sprinkle the cornmeal over the water. Continue to stir constantly for 2 to 3 minutes, or until the mixture is thick and smooth.

3. While the water is heating, in a small bowl, combine the butter and oil and stir until well mixed. When you remove the cornmeal batter from the heat, add the butter-oil mixture, honey, and salt and stir until combined. Let the batter cool for 2 to 3 minutes, or until you can stick your finger in it and leave it there for at least 5 seconds.

4. Add the milk and beaten eggs and egg whites to the batter and beat well with a whisk or handheld electric mixer on medium speed for about 2 minutes, or until smooth and well incorporated. The batter will be thin.

5. Spray an 8- or 9-inch ovenproof cast-iron or other heavy skillet with vegetable oil spray, or wipe it with a paper towel that has been dipped in grapeseed oil. Heat the skillet over medium heat for 5 to 8 minutes, or until almost hot. Pour the batter into the pan and transfer it to the oven. Bake for about 20 minutes, or until the spoon bread stops puffing and rising. Do not overcook.

6. Remove the pan from the oven and very gently fan the pear slices over the spoon bread in a circular pattern. Sprinkle with the cinnamon and return to the oven for about 10 minutes, or until nicely browned. The pears will be tender and still hold their shape.

7. Remove the spoon bread from the oven and spoon the warm glaze over it. Serve right away directly from the pan.

NOTE: It's crucial to use stone-ground cornmeal for this spoonbread. If you mistakenly buy a cornmeal mix or meal that is not stone ground, the spoonbread may be tough and hard. Also, take care you don't overcook the cornmeal batter.

cranberry, orange, and jalapeño glaze

MAKES ABOUT
1
CUP

THIS GLAZE IS ONE OF MY FAVORITE USES FOR FRESH CRANBERRIES. I live in the Northeast, where cranberries abound and I look forward to them every fall. Teamed with fresh juices and heated up with a jalapeño, the berries form a magnificent glaze for the pear tart.

Sadly, countless cranberry farmers are going out of business because their crop has been relegated to a very narrow portion of the food industry: cranberry juice and once-a-year canned relish. Cranberries are one of the best natural antioxidants you can consume. So, help yourself and the farmers and eat more cranberries!

2 CUPS FRESHLY PRESSED APPLE JUICE or apple cider, plus more if needed

2 CUPS FRESH ORANGE JUICE, plus more if needed

½ CUP CRANBERRIES, well rinsed

ONE 3-INCH-LONG CINNAMON STICK (see Note)

½ VANILLA BEAN

1 JALAPEÑO CHILI, halved lengthwise

SALT

LOCAL HONEY, if needed

1. In a saucepan, combine the 2 cups each apple juice and orange juice and the cranberries and bring to a boil over medium-high heat.

2. Meanwhile, holding the cinnamon stick with tongs, toast it an inch or so above a high gas flame for about 1 minute, or until it darkens a shade and is fragrant. You can also set it directly on a hot electric coil and turn it as it toasts. This takes 20 to 30 seconds. With either method, be sure to wear oven mitts or use a reliable pot holder.

3. Add the cinnamon stick, vanilla bean, and jalapeño to the simmering cranberries. Stir gently just to mix. Simmer gently, uncovered, for about 1¼ hours, or until the cranberries are soft and the liquid is syrupy and measures about 1 cup. If the liquid evaporates, moisten the cranberries by adding small, equal amounts of apple and orange juice.

4. Pluck out and discard the cinnamon stick, jalapeño, and vanilla bean. Season the glaze to taste with salt and, if necessary, honey. (Honey is most healthful if not overheated, so allow the glaze to cool a little before adding any honey.) Use immediately or keep warm until needed.

NOTE: I don't always specify a length for the cinnamon sticks I use, but here because the cinnamon is in the glaze for more than an hour, I suggest you use one no more than 3 inches long.

Sweet Corn and Toasted Almond
RICE PUDDING

SERVES
8

I'VE GOTTEN A LOT OF POSITIVE ATTENTION FOR MY SWEET CORN SAUCE, which is a lynchpin of my well-being cuisine. It's made from pure corn juice and tastes like summer's best sweet corn eaten right off the cob, times twelve! The juice thickens itself as it heats because it contains natural cornstarch, so no other ingredients that might interfere with the purity and sweetness of the corn are necessary. I have surrendered further to the amazing sweetness of corn by allowing it to become dessert!

This pudding is egg-free and is healthful, even though I add a little heavy cream. With only a little more than a tablespoon of cream per serving, the dessert contains far less fat than the typical rice pudding. Corn and vanilla are fond of each other and pair magically here, and the honey and tiny bit of salt compensate for the blandness of the rice. I like to use sushi rice,

which is short grain and starchy and thus sticky enough to work with the corn juice to give the pudding a custardlike consistency. Top the pudding with toasted almonds and some raw cane sugar browned brûlée style, and you have a dessert to remember.

continued

1 CUP SLIVERED BLANCHED ALMONDS

2 CUPS WARM, COOKED SUSHI RICE

1 CUP CREAMY SWEET CORN SAUCE (page 208)

2 TABLESPOONS GRATED LEMON ZEST

1 VANILLA BEAN, split lengthwise, or ½ teaspoon pure almond or vanilla extract

1 TEASPOON FINE SEA SALT, plus more if needed

½ CUP HEAVY CREAM

2 TABLESPOONS LOCAL HONEY

2 TO 3 TABLESPOONS RAW CANE SUGAR

1. Preheat the oven to 375°F.

2. Spread the almonds on a baking sheet and toast in the oven, stirring once, for 3 to 5 minutes, or until lightly browned and fragrant. Pour onto a plate to cool. Set aside.

3. In a saucepan, stir together the warm rice, corn sauce, lemon zest, vanilla bean (if using extract, add it later), and salt. Fold in about three-fourths of the toasted almonds, reserving the rest to sprinkle over the puddings. Taste and add up to ½ teaspoon more salt, if needed. Cook over medium heat, stirring constantly, for about 3 minutes, or until the pudding is cooked through and the flavors blend. Transfer to a bowl, stir in the vanilla extract (if using) and let cool to room temperature.

4. Using a handheld electric mixer or a wire whisk, whip the cream until it begins to form soft peaks. Add the honey and continue whipping until it reaches stiff peaks. Gently fold the whipped cream into the cooled rice pudding.

5. If you used a vanilla bean, remove and discard it. Divide the pudding among eight ¾-cup ovenproof ramekins or custard cups. Cover each ramekin with plastic wrap and refrigerate for at least 2 hours, or until thoroughly chilled.

6. Preheat the broiler or have ready a kitchen-sized butane torch.

7. Remove the plastic wrap from the puddings and arrange the ramekins on a baking sheet. Top each pudding with the reserved toasted almonds and then sprinkle with a light, even coating of the sugar.

8. Slip the puddings under the broiler about 4 inches from the heating element for 30 to 50 seconds, or until the sugar forms a crisp, lightly browned glaze. Alternatively, use the torch, running it evenly over the surface of each pudding just until lightly browned. Serve at once.

creamy sweet corn sauce

MAKES ABOUT
1½
CUPS

WHEN I BEGAN MY JOURNEY TO CREATE HEALTHFUL MENUS, I was daunted by the idea of trying to make sauces without such classic thickening agents as roux, processed cornstarch, arrowroot, and reduced cream. Because I juice a lot, I wondered if the juice from vegetables that contain natural starches might thicken on their own when heated. I began with corn because I like it so much and it was plentiful in the late summer when I started to experiment. Much to my personal joy, it worked beautifully! And it's been among my favorites ever since. Over time, I found it thickened even further when refrigerated, which made it perfect for binding crab cakes (hooray!), for flavoring salad dressings, and for naturally sweetening desserts.

6 CUPS CORN KERNELS
(from 8 or 9 ears)

1 TO 2 TABLESPOONS
FRESH LEMON JUICE

SALT AND FRESHLY GROUND
BLACK PEPPER

I. Juice the corn kernels in a heavy-duty juicer. You should have 1½ to 2 cups corn juice.

2. Put the corn juice in the top pan of a double boiler and heat over (but not touching) gently simmering water, stirring constantly to prevent simmering, for 4 to 6 minutes, or until thickened, slightly frothy, and smooth. If the sauce simmers, it may curdle. If you stop stirring, it may break and will not be retrievable.

3. Remove the sauce from the heat and strain through a fine-mesh sieve. Season to taste with lemon juice, salt, and pepper.

4. Use immediately, or cover and refrigerate for up to 5 days. The sauce can be served warm or cold. To reheat the refrigerated sauce, pour into a double boiler over gently simmering water and heat, stirring constantly to prevent curdling, for 6 to 8 minutes.

ANGEL FOOD CAKE

SERVES
12 TO **16**

WHILE MOST OF MY RECIPES DO NOT CALL FOR PROCESSED SUGAR AND FLOUR, there is no denying the technical advances in baking that these ingredients have allowed. And then there is the reality that many of us carefully watch what we eat throughout the day so that we can indulge in ice cream or cake at day's end. With two diabetic sons, Chris and Ethan, I've shunned cakes for years because of the double-whammy of refined sugar and flour.

Inevitably, there are times when nothing else will do but a cake. And why not? I only serve cake at the end of a healthful meal and, it goes without saying, the cake has to be an outstanding one. When I was constructing menus at New York's Heartbeat, where I was executive chef for several years, I labeled half of the desserts *indulgences.* This recipe is definitely an indulgence.

Up until now, you have been cooking the healthful savory recipes on these pages, but with this recipe, I will *indulge* you with the dessert my siblings and I loved more than any other when we were kids. By the time I was halfway home from school, I could tell my mom was baking angel food cake because the vanilla-almond scent perfumed the entire neighborhood. On the downside, we had to wait until supper was over to eat the irresistible cake (not that Mom's meals were downers).

The extremely simple recipe is inspired by one that appears in the old *Buckeye Cookbook,* which was passed to me by Mom, and to her by her mother. The book is so old that it still uses measurements such as tumblers and gills, but I have translated them for contemporary kitchens. For a lighter cake, use all cake flour and add ½ teaspoon almond extract. If possible, use an

angel food cake pan, which has a center tube and a removable bottom. Do not grease the pan, or the cake will not cling to the tube and sides and thus rise properly. Never open the oven door during the first half hour of baking. The light batter requires constant heat to rise. The reward is unforgettable. Serve the cake with fresh berries or sliced fruit. I especially like it with summer's juiciest peaches. You can also top it with sweetened whipped cream.

Aside from a darned tasty cake, there is an extra-added bonus for any leftovers. Make what I call Panfried Angel Food Cake (page 214). Now, there's an indulgent indulgence!

continued

1 CUP CAKE FLOUR (see Note)

¼ CUP ALMOND FLOUR
(see Note)

¼ TEASPOON SALT

1½ CUPS EGG WHITES
(10 to 11 large eggs)

1 TEASPOON CREAM OF TARTAR

1¾ CUPS VANILLA BEAN SUGAR
(recipe follows), sifted

NOTE: Cake flour is milled from soft wheat, which simply means it is low in protein and thus produces a soft, tender crumb. Some brands include leaveners (baking soda and baking powder) and are called self-rising flour. Do *not* use self-rising cake flour here.

Almond flour is finely ground blanched almonds. It is easy to make your own if you have a food processor or powerful blender, and I recommend it for such a small amount and for the best almond flavor. For the ¼ cup needed here, you will need about 1 ounce slivered blanched almonds. I suggest mixing them with a teaspoon or so of the cake flour when you grind it to keep it from clumping. You can also buy it in specialty stores and well-stocked natural-foods markets. Like other nut flours, it does not keep well and should be used within a week or two.

1. Preheat the oven to 250°F.

2. Sift together the cake flour and almond flour 4 times. Add the salt and then sift again.

3. In the clean, dry bowl of an electric mixer fitted with a clean, dry whip attachment, whip the egg whites until very foamy. Add the cream of tartar and continue beating until stiff peaks form. You also can do this by hand, using a balloon whisk and a large, wide bowl or large, deep platter.

4. With the mixer running, slowly and gently beat in the sugar. Immediately add the sifted dry ingredients and mix just until combined.

5. Pour the batter into an ungreased 10-inch angel food cake pan with a removable bottom. If you don't have an angel food cake pan, you can use a Bundt pan or similar tube pan. As you scrape the batter into the pan, keep mixing it with a rubber spatula, as some of the flour will have sunk to the bottom of the bowl.

6. Put the pan in the oven, then, as soon as you close the oven door, raise the temperature to 325°F. Do *not* open the oven door for at least 15 minutes so that the cake can begin rising. Bake for 45 to 55 minutes, or until the cake is nicely browned and a toothpick inserted halfway between the rim and the center tube comes out clean.

7. Remove the cake from the oven and immediately invert the pan to cool. Leave it inverted until cool, or for at least 1 hour. Angel food cake pans are fitted with little feet that hold the pan above the countertop when inverted. This promotes good air circulation. If you are using a Bundt or other tube pan, invert it over the neck of a wine bottle.

8. When the cake has cooled to room temperature, remove it from the pan, using a very thin metal spatula to loosen any stubborn areas. Traditionally, angel food cakes are gently torn apart with a large fork designed for the task, or cut with a serrated knife.

vanilla bean sugar

MAKES
4
CUPS

MOM COULDN'T RESIST ADDING HER OWN TOUCH TO JUST ABOUT EVERYTHING. Whether it was embellishing already-decorated Christmas tree ornaments with fresh paint or "spiking" granulated sugar with lemon verbena and vanilla, nothing escaped her touch. I think this was her way of teaching her kids to be creative.

I FRESH LEMON VERBENA SPRIG, 9 or 10 inches long, cut into 3-inch lengths (see page 47)

4 CUPS GRANULATED SUGAR

3 VANILLA BEANS, split lengthwise

I. Stack the verbena lengths in a glass container large enough to hold all the sugar. Pour about 2 cups of the sugar into the container. Stick the split vanilla beans into the sugar and then cover with the remaining sugar.

2. Seal the jar tightly and store for at least 1 week. Once the sugar is as aromatic as you like, strain out the vanilla and verbena. You can reuse the vanilla beans to perfume more sugar.

Panfried
ANGEL FOOD CAKE

SERVES
4

FRESHLY BAKED AND COOLED ANGEL FOOD CAKE IS JUST AS THE NAME IMPLIES—*HEAVENLY!* Unfortunately, the texture changes dramatically a day or two after the cake is baked. My mother stretched leftovers of this awesome cake by panfrying it.

Panfried cake slices are great with puréed berries, local honey, or homemade savory jams (my favorite). The skill level for this is about the same as for a grilled cheese sandwich, which means anyone can make this indulgence. The tough part is that you can't leave it unattended. As with a grilled cheese sandwich, if you turn your back for even a few seconds too long, all can be lost. You will smell your mistake before you see it. Be attentive!

3 TABLESPOONS UNSALTED BUTTER, at soft room temperature

4 SLICES LEFTOVER ANGEL FOOD CAKE (page 209), each about 1 inch thick

2 TO 3 TABLESPOONS LOCAL HONEY or one of the jams in the Extending the Harvest chapter (page 144)

1. Lightly butter each side of the cake slices. Lay the slices in a nonstick skillet and panfry over medium-high heat for about 2 minutes, or until golden brown on the bottom. Turn the slices and fry until lightly browned on the other side.

2. Transfer each slice to a plate and immediately drizzle with honey. If you want to use jam, I recommend dumping it into the hot pan off the heat, stirring until it melts, and then spooning it over the cake slices. This recipe is *succulenté!*

Cardamom-Strawberry
SHORT BISCUITS
with Clabbered Cream

**SERVES
8**

NO QUESTION ABOUT IT, THIS IS AN INDULGENT RECIPE. Since I began my journey toward well-being, I rarely turn to butter or full-fat dairy products, but there are times when these luscious products have a place even at the most healthful meal. If you can buy milk, cream, and cheese from a small dairy, you will likely purchase a superior product that has not been overprocessed and that tastes fresh and sweet. This is especially true if you can find dairy products that have not been homogenized. Plus, you will be supporting local agriculture and farmers, always a good idea, and you will glean the health benefits, too. It's a win-win situation. On the West Coast, I like Cowgirl Creamery based in Point Reyes Station near San Francisco, and on the East Coast, I look for Ronnybrook Farm products, which are sold in a number of small markets. Ronnybrook Farm is located in New

York's glorious Hudson Valley in a small town called Ancramdale. Organic Valley Farms produces my pick for the best widely available milk.

This is my version of strawberry shortcake, everyone's favorite summertime dessert, but with some obvious differences. I bake biscuits made with both white and whole-wheat flour and flavored with cardamom, a spice I fell in love with years ago when a South Asian cook working in my kitchen introduced me to it. It behaves a little like cinnamon in that its clear, identifiable flavor works across a spectrum of sweet and savory tastes. I also use local honey to flavor both the biscuits and the berries.

While I grow many vegetables, I don't grow berries. Luckily, my neighbor Bob Connelly is into berries, so he supplies me with the fruit and I supply him with vegetables and herbs. This is

continued

cardamom-strawberry short biscuits with clabbered cream

continued

an example of how gardening can become a community effort, in either an informal way, as with Bob and me, or a more organized system, as with community gardens. Bob must have a hundred blueberry bushes in his front and side yard. He never uses all the berries, but there are so many that the birds get their fill, too. Allowing birds into your berry patch is good for the garden because birds are great for cross-pollination. But if you have only a few plants, the birds will wipe you out.

All you need for blueberry bushes or straw-berry beds is a little sunny land. Plant the bushes along the side of the house in place of azaleas or rhododendrons. If you don't have Bob's energy or the luxury of his space, you will plant far fewer bushes. Protect them from the birds with protective netting, such as light, manageable nylon deer-fencing material. You won't regret it!

STRAWBERRIES

8 PINTS VERY RIPE STRAWBERRIES

½ **CUP LOCAL HONEY**

¼ **VANILLA BEAN,** split lengthwise

2 TABLESPOONS GRATED LEMON ZEST

24 FRESH LEMON VERBENA LEAVES (see page 47)

CARDAMOM SHORT BISCUITS

4 GREEN CARDAMOM PODS

2½ **CUPS WHOLE-WHEAT FLOUR**

1½ **CUPS UNBLEACHED ALL-PURPOSE FLOUR**

2 TABLESPOONS BAKING POWDER

1 TEASPOON PLUS 1 PINCH FINE SEA SALT

¾ **CUP FROZEN UNSALTED BUTTER**

4 TABLESPOONS FROZEN LARD

2 LARGE EGGS, lightly beaten

1 CUP WHOLE MILK

¼ **CUP SOUR CREAM**

⅓ **CUP LOCAL HONEY**

continued

1. To prepare the strawberries, hull all the berries. Chop 2 pints of the berries and set aside. Halve the remaining 6 pints of berries, transfer to a bowl, cover with a lightly dampened paper towel, and keep at room temperature.

2. Put half of the chopped berries in a saucepan, add the honey, vanilla bean, lemon zest, and lemon verbena leaves, and bring to a simmer over medium heat. Cook gently for about 15 minutes, or until reduced by one-third, thickened, and saucy. Set aside to cool.

3. Transfer the remaining chopped berries to a food processor and add the cooled berries. Remove and discard the vanilla bean. Process briefly, just until smooth. You will have about 2 cups sauce. Cover and refrigerate until needed.

4. To make the biscuits, preheat the oven to 425°F.

5. In a small, dry skillet, toast the cardamom pods over medium-high heat, shaking the pan occasionally, for 3 to 5 minutes, or until lightly browned on all sides. Remove from the heat, let cool, and then grind in a spice grinder, a coffee grinder reserved for spices, or in a mortar with a pestle. You will have about ¼ teaspoon ground cardamom.

6. In a large bowl, stir together the flours, baking powder, ground cardamom, and salt.

7. Using the large holes on a handheld grater, grate the frozen butter and lard into the dry ingredients. (I hold the fats directly over the bowl and wear a double layer of latex gloves to protect my fingers from the grater.) Using a fork, cut the fats into the dry ingredients until you have a coarse mixture with lumps about the size of peas.

8. In another bowl, whisk together the eggs, milk, and sour cream until blended. Pour into the flour mixture and then drizzle in the honey. Mix the ingredients together with a fork just until the dough begins to come together in large globs or clumps. The less you mix the biscuit dough, the more tender the biscuits will be.

9. Turn the dough out onto a lightly floured surface and knead gently just until it comes together. With lightly buttered hands, press the dough into a square or rectangle ¾ to 1 inch thick. Flour a sharp knife and cut the dough into rough 2½-inch squares or diamonds. You should have enough dough for 12 biscuits.

continued

TOPPING

2 TABLESPOONS UNSALTED BUTTER, melted

2 TABLESPOONS LOCAL HONEY, warmed

2 TABLESPOONS RAW CANE SUGAR

1½ **CUPS CLABBERED CREAM** (see Note)

12 FRESH LEMON VERBENA SPRIGS

10. Put the biscuits on an ungreased rimmed baking sheet or a sheet lined with parchment paper, spacing them about 1 inch apart. Bake for 6 minutes.

11. Meanwhile, make the topping. In a small bowl, mix together the melted butter and warm honey. When the biscuits have baked for 6 minutes, remove them from the oven and brush with the honey-butter. Sprinkle each biscuit with the sugar. Return the biscuits to the oven and bake for 6 to 9 minutes longer, or until the tops are light golden brown. Do not let them brown further.

12. Transfer the biscuits to wire racks and let cool just until you can handle them comfortably. Split the warm biscuits with your fingers for a rustic look, and put the bottom of each biscuit, "cut side" up, on a dessert plate. Drizzle a little strawberry sauce on each biscuit bottom and then top with the room-temperature halved strawberries. Drizzle with more sauce, top with clabbered cream, and then the top half of the biscuit. Serve garnished with the lemon verbena sprigs.

NOTE: If you can't find clabbered cream, substitute crème fraîche, English Devonshire cream, or whipped cream. For more information on clabbered cream, see the Glossary on the facing page.

GLOSSARY

CARDAMOM: An intensely flavored and aromatic spice, cardamom is used principally in curries and in baked goods. It is sold as seed-filled pods or ground, with two primary types available, green, the most commonly used, and black, which has a more rustic flavor. The purchased ground spice lacks the pungency possible when you grind your own in a mortar and pestle or spice grinder. The entire pod or just the seeds can be ground. The choice depends on the recipe.

CHAAT MASALA: *See* masala spice.

CHILI POWDER: Most commercial chili powders are compounds made up of ground dried chilies, cumin, oregano, garlic, coriander, and cloves, and they are used to flavor chili (the stew), egg dishes, tuna salads, and more. Pure ancho chili powder is made from ground ancho chilies and has a different—and some would say better—flavor than most pure chili powders or compound powders. I like to use ancho chili powder, which is sold in Latin markets and many gourmet stores, but use the kind you like best. Always seek high-quality powders for their superior flavor.

CIPOLLINI ONIONS: These small, flat yellow onions are similar to pearl onions and have a sweet, mild flavor. Peel before cooking.

CLABBERED CREAM: Sometimes called thick milk, clabbered cream is the thick, slightly curdled milk—almost the consistency of whipped cream—that traditionally rises to the top of milk before it is homogenized. It's hard to find because most of the milk sold in this country is pasteurized and homogenized. Depending on the recipe, you can use crème fraîche, British clotted cream, Devonshire cream, or whipped cream in its place.

EDAMAME: These are green soybeans sold fresh in the shell and sold frozen both shelled and unshelled. The fresh beans require slightly shorter cooking time than the thawed, frozen ones and are harder to find. The frozen product, sold in Asian markets and well-stocked supermarkets in regions of the country with large Asian populations, is excellent.

FAVA BEANS: These shell beans, which resemble large lima beans, are sold fresh in the pod and frozen both in the pod and shelled. Fresh shelled favas are covered with a thin, somewhat tough, bitter skin that must be removed before the beans are cooked. Blanch the beans briefly in boiling water, drain, and slip off the skins. They will come off easily. Very young, tender fava beans do not need peeling.

FLEUR DE SEL: One of the most expensive salts, fleur de sel is harvested by hand in France. It is made from the crust that forms on the surface of some salt beds, and it is sparkling white because it never comes in contact with dark natural material at the bottom of the beds. It is used principally as a condiment for sprinkling on foods just before eating. *See also* sea salt.

FRESH BAY LEAVES: Fresh bay laurel leaves impart a lovely, sweet flavor that cannot be compared to the flavor of their dried counterparts. Bay laurel plants are easy to grow and are increasingly sold alongside other fresh herbs plants. They flourish inside and can be overwintered in most climates. Use fresh basil leaves if you cannot find fresh bay leaves.

GARAM MASALA: This blend of Indian spices usually includes black pepper, mace, cinnamon, cumin, and nutmeg. Garam masala is typically added to a dish either just before or just after it has finished cooking. The gourmet sections of some supermarkets carry garam masala, but the best blends are found in Indian markets. *See also* masala spice.

GRAPESEED OIL: Grapeseed oil is the oil of choice for many of my recipes. Unlike olive oil, it does not thicken in the refrigerator and its flavor is more subtle. If you only have olive oil, or prefer it, the finished dish will still taste wonderful.

HABANERO CHILI PEPPER: This lantern-shaped pepper is reputedly the world's hottest chili. It is typically about 2 inches long and 1½ inches in diameter, and ranges from a deep green to a bright orange or bright red when fully ripe. You can use any hot chili pepper for these, depending on the degree of heat you like. Be careful handling these as they can burn. Do not touch your mouth or eyes while working with them.

HAM HOCK: From the lower part of a ham, the hock is primarily used to flavor soups and stews, although it has good-sized pieces of meat and fat. Fresh hocks are rarely available (you may need to special order them), but smoked ham hocks are easy to find in supermarkets and butcher shops.

HEIRLOOM TOMATOES: These nonhybrid species tend to be better tasting than hybrids, but are also more expensive and harder to find. Specialty farmers' markets or specialty produce markets carry them along with other heirloom produce. If a recipe calls for a particular heirloom tomato and you cannot find it, substitute another. Otherwise, use vine-ripened tomatoes of any kind.

JAGGERY: This typically Indian sweetener is made by dehydrating cane sugar juice. In some parts of India, it might be made from palm sugar. It adds a beautiful rustic sweetness to dishes and is not easy to substitute. If you cannot find it, use light brown or Demerara sugar. Look for jaggery in Indian markets, or order by mail (see Sources, facing page).

LEMONGRASS: A flavorful herb from Southeast Asia, lemongrass has a long, woody leaves and a slightly enlarged base reminiscent of a scallion base. It is sold in Asian markets and some supermarkets. Cut off and discard the leafy tops, and then peel off the tough outer layers of the base before using.

MASALA SPICE: Masala is any Indian spice mixture. Such mixtures are available in Indian markets and online (see Sources, facing page). Variations of masala spice mixtures exist, such as garam masala, chaat masala, goda masala, and tandoori masala; most contain cardamom, cinnamon, cumin, cloves, nutmeg, and peppercorns. *See also* garam masala.

MEYER LEMON: Commonly believed to be a cross between a lemon and an orange or mandarin orange, Meyer lemons taste slightly sweeter and are larger and rounder than regular lemons. They have a yellow-orange tint and a thin skin. Most Meyer lemons are grown in California and can be hard to find outside the state. Use mild grapefruit or regular lemons instead.

PANEER: This mildly flavored, fresh cow's milk cheese is sold in Indian markets. If you cannot find it, use buffalo mozzarella cheese in its place. You can also make your own paneer: For 1 cup paneer, bring 2 cups whole milk to a boil, remove from the heat, and add 2 or 3 tablespoons fresh lemon juice. You need enough lemon juice to curdle the milk. When the curds separate from the whey (that is, the milk curdles), let sit for a few minutes and then pour into a cheesecloth-lined sieve. The solids (curds) are the paneer. Place the paneer in a dish, cover with a cloth, and weight with a heavy pan or similar object for several hours or until firm enough to cut. The cheese will keep in the refrigerator for up to 4 days.

RAW CANE SUGAR: Raw cane sugar is metabolized more slowly in the body than granulated sugar. Plus, by the virtue of being less processed, it's kinder to the earth. Look for supermarket brands such as Dixie Crystals and Sugar in the Raw, or products labeled Florida cane sugar.

RAZ AL HANOUT: It literally means "head of the shop" and is pronounced *rasal ha-noot*. A blending of dry spices, it is used liberally in the cuisines of Morocco, Tunisia, and Turkey, and can be likened to India's garam masala, in that every home cook and restaurant chef has his or her own favorite and even the store-bought mixes are never uniform. Commonly used with rice, couscous, and stews, it usually contains peppercorns, cardamom, mace, nutmeg, and cinnamon. Look for it in North African and Middle Eastern markets.

RICE OIL: Also called rice bran oil, this exceptionally nutritious oil is light and versatile and has a mild, pleasing flavor. Use it for cooking or for vinaigrettes. Not many stores stock it, so you may have to order it from the California Rice Oil Company (see Sources, facing page).

SEA SALT: This salt is harvested from the sea and is appreciated for its pleasingly strong taste and crystalline texture. Both coarse and fine sea salts are sold. I use coarse sea salt unless otherwise specified. I like the salt packaged by the Maine Sea Salt Company, which sells a natural, sun-dried sea salt from the nutrient- and mineral-rich Gulf of Maine. *See also* fleur de sel.

SOBA NOODLES: Sometimes called buckwheat soba noodles, these Japanese noodles are made from buckwheat flour mixed with wheat flour. The buckwheat makes them beige and gives them a nutty flavor and slightly chewy texture. In Japan, chefs take great pride in their ability to make soba noodles, and surely they are at their best when fresh. Dried soba noodles are sold in Asian markets and, increasingly, in supermarkets.

STAR ANISE: The segmented star-shaped seedpod of a Chinese evergreen, star anise has a flavor close to, although more bitter than, traditional anise. Look for it in Asian markets, specialty-foods stores, and some supermarkets.

SUMAC: The berries of the sumac bush are sold dried whole or ground for use as a spice. Sumac complements seafood, poultry, lamb, and vegetables with a fruity, yet sour flavor. Look for it in Middle Eastern markets.

THAI CHILI PEPPER: Also known as bird chili, this diminutive, extremely hot pepper carries heat that holds on through the cooking process. Thai chilies can be green or red and measure about 1 inch long. They are available in supermarkets and Asian markets. Substitute jalapeño, serrano, or pequin chilies.

SOURCES

Here are some places to find some harder-to-find and specialty products.

ANSON MILLS
ansonmills.com
1922-C Gervais Street
Columbia, South Carolina 29201
Tel: 803-467-4122
Fax: 803-256-2463
Small-batch flour, cornmeal, grits, semolina, and polenta

BOB'S RED MILL NATURAL FOODS
bobsredmill.com
5209 SE International Way
Milwaukie, Oregon 97222
Tel: 800-349-2173
Organic whole-grain flours and baking supplies

CALIFORNIA RICE OIL COMPANY
californiariceoil.com
Double 7 Products Inc.
138-H Hamilton Drive
Novato, California 94949
Tel: 415-382-0373
Fax: 415-382-0297
Rice oil

COAST OF MAINE ORGANIC PRODUCTS, INC.
coastofmaine.com
145 Newbury Street
Portland, Maine 04101
Tel: 800-345-9315
Fax: 207-879-0554
Organic garden products including loam, peat, and fertilizer

COWGIRL CREAMERY
cowgirlcreamery.com
P.O. Box 594
80 Fourth Street
Point Reyes Station, California 94956
Tel: 415-663-9335
Fax: 415-663-5418
Source information for organic milk and other organic dairy products

HERITAGE FOODS USA
heritagefoodsusa.com
P.O. Box 827
New York, New York 10150
Tel: 212-980-6603
Fax: 212-980-6603
Responsibly raised meat and poultry, wild rice, and other organic and artisanal foodstuffs

IROQUOIS WHITE CORN
bioneers.org
Iroquois corn flour, tamal flour, and hominy

KALUSTYANS
kalustyans.com
123 Lexington Avenue
New York, New York 10016
Tel: 212-685-3451
Fax: 212-683-8458
Spices and seasonings, including Middle Eastern and Indian spices

MAINE SEA SALT
maineseasalt.com
10 Barrows Drive
Topsham, Maine 04086
Tel: 207-725-5415
Sea salt, flavored sea salt, and dulse seaweed

NATIVE SEEDS/SEARCH
nativeseeds.org
526 North Fourth Avenue
Tucson, Arizona 85705
Tel: 520-622-5561
Fax: 520-622-5591
Heirloom and other hard-to-find garden seeds

ORGANIC VALLEY FAMILY OF FARMS
organicvalley.com
One Organic Way
LaFarge, Wisconsin 54639
Tel: 888-444-6455
Fax: 608-625-2600
Source information for organic milk and other organic dairy products

NIMAN RANCH
nimanranch.com
1025 East Twelfth Street
Oakland, California 94606
Tel: 510-808-0340
Responsibly raised beef, lamb, and pork

PENZEYS
penzeys.com
Tel: 800-741-77787
Fax: 262-785-7678
Spices and seasonings, including Middle Eastern, North African, and Indian spices, as well as others

SANKOW'S BEAVER BROOK FARM
beaverbrookfarm.com
139 Beaver Brook Road
Lyme, Connecticut 06371
Tel: 860-434-2843
Artisan lamb, milk and cheese products

SEEDS OF CHANGE
seedsofchange.com
Tel: 888-762-7333
Heirloom and other hard-to-find garden seeds

STONYFIELD FARM ORGANIC YOGURT
stonyfield.com
Ten Burton Drive
Londonderry, New Hampshire 03053
Tel: 800-776-2697
Organic yogurt and yogurt products

SWEET PEET
sweetpeet.com
Salem Organic Soils
P.O. Box 352
Wingdale, New York 12594
Tel: 800-725-5360
Organic garden products, including loam, peat, and fertilizer

TEN REN TEA COMPANY
tenren.com
419 Eccles Avenue
South San Francisco, California 94080
Tel: 650-583-1047
High-quality specialty teas

FOR QUALITY INFORMATION ON MAKING SUSTAINABLE FOOD CHOICES, GO TO THESE WEB SITES:

ANIMAL WELFARE INSTITUTE
awionline.org

BIONEERS
bioneers.org

BLUE OCEAN INSTITUTE
blueoceaninstitute.org

CENTER FOR HEALTH AND THE GLOBAL ENVIRONMENT
med.harvard.edu

EARTH PLEDGE FOUNDATION
earthpledge.org

FARM AID
farmaid.org

GLYNNWOOD CENTER
glynwood.org

THE LEOPOLD CENTER FOR SUSTAINABLE AGRICULTURE
leopold.iastate.edu

MONTEREY BAY AQUARIUM RESEARCH INSTITUTE
mbari.org

TOHONO O'ODHAM COMMUNITY ACTION
tocaonline.org

W. K. KELLOGG FOUNDATION
wkkf.org

ACKNOWLEDGMENTS

HOMEGROWN PURE AND SIMPLE
Dedication to the Journey of Many a Family

MY MOVE TOWARD COOKING FOR WELL-BEING WAS DRIVEN BY MY FIRST SON'S DIAGNOSIS OF INSULIN-DEPENDENT DIABETES. Chris's disease helped me understand that, for millions who suffer common health conditions, the simple act of choosing a cookbook or reading a menu is an exercise in being reminded of all the things you cannot have. Since *Taste: Pure and Simple*, my first book, was published, my youngest son, Ethan, was also diagnosed with insulin-dependent diabetes. The direction of my work is now informed in a deeper, more poignant way.

Many folks ask my wife, Lori, and me how we can possibly handle such an unfair burden. We remind them that many families have it far worse. The tough truth is that thousands of families deal with a variety of health-related circumstances such as rare blood disorders, childhood and adult cancers, liver disease, and others that will indeed rob them of their loved ones at a time when they are both the most and the least prepared. Because diabetes is treatable with proper insulin management, those who suffer from it can lead a long, fairly healthy life. For this, we count ourselves lucky.

Privately, though, we understand the terrible truth of this potentially ravaging disease. I find it in Lori's eyes when she holds Ethan tight while he sleeps, in her trembling arms when she comforts him after a seizure, in her pain-filled voice every time his or Chris's glucose levels are inexplicably high, in the way she caresses Chris's teenage hair while he sleeps as though he is still just five years old. We know that by the time they reach their thirties, they each will have had diabetes for well over two decades. We understand, too well, that proper insulin management is no guarantee that we will not part with our beloved sons earlier than we would wish.

The sad truth is that, to a great extent, most of the disorders I have mentioned may be preventable by changing the way we treat our environment and our food supply. The majority of all cancers and immune disorders may be environmentally caused. The way humans treat the environment is at the root of these diseases, and there is no worse example of this terrible truth than in how we annually dump millions of tons of toxins into our food supply.

Ironically, there is also no better example of hope than that which comes from the same food supply. Changing the way we buy, grow, and prepare our food is where the rubber meets the road when it comes to ensuring a healthful future for our children and our environment. The happy truth is that if we achieve meaningful change, the future will be a better place. Nature is self-healing in ways that have confounded humans since the dawn of time.

So, we do need to change, if only a little at a time. One less meal at a fast-food restaurant this week multiplied by several million families equals significant change. One organically grown apple per day, per child, per average household will not break the budget but it will change the apple industry. This is an example of how the simplest family from Anywhere USA can be true heroes and make a true difference. No one should ever feel he or she has to buy all organic to make a difference. It is just this sort of hogwash that prevents many a strapped family from buying a half dozen organic apples, even when the rest of their purchases are nonorganic.

For those who think you're evil if you stop at the drive-through, here's some food for thought. Michel Nischan eat fast food? Guilty as charged. Michel Nischan's kids eat Taco Bell? Guilty as charged. Michel Nischan serve farm-raised salmon or work for a major cola company? Guilty as charged. Michel Nischan buy nonorganic food for his family? Guilty as charged (and, for years, no choice in the matter). Michel Nischan and family do something about it in more recent years by reducing visits to the drive-though, buying local apples at the farmstand, and planting an organic garden? Guilty as charged.

My family and I have been trapped in the same system of cost and convenience as everyone else. While we have always supported local farmers and tried to eat as well as we could, like so many other families, we often lived paycheck-to-paycheck. Still, over time, we have been slowly changing the way we buy and eat our food. In doing so, we have continually found ways to make a difference and to eat better. While it is unfortunate that it was Chris's diagnosis more than ten years ago that drove the point home, it has undeniably caused an unstoppable forward momentum.

This same momentum is my prayer for everyone, though not because of a significant emotional event such as ours. In fact, I pray that folks who are blessed with good health and healthy families don't wait for "something bad to happen." Everyone should start now to eat more healthfully and assume some stewardship for our good earth. A single apple or glass of organic milk in the hands of many will affect the future. If we take the small steps to change the way we buy our food, those we buy our food from will likely change the way they raise our food.

If we can grow our own food, even if it's only some herbs in a windowbox or cherry tomatoes on the patio, we can help our children understand that poetry lives in a single fragrant leaf. And if we can understand that such fragrance is created by things that can actually enhance our well-being, we and our children can begin to understand why the words "you are what you eat" should never be disregarded as a cliché.

DEDICATION TO MY FAMILY

CHRIS and ETHAN, your courage is greater than mine will ever be. I wish I could take your illnesses on myself so that you could live your lives without the invasion of another needle or pin. You make me who I am. Thanks from the bottom of my heart.

LAUREN and COURTNEY, you drive me crazy! Your teenage ways drive me crazy and humble me all at once. After all, I was once the same. All of your actions, though, help me understand that karma truly exists, that there is indeed a God, and that Mom and Dad (rest their souls) are looking on and laughing heartily at the spectacle! And when I see the look in your eyes when you play with little Drew and littler Ethan, I know the love in your hearts runs deep and that your souls are good and true. God, how I love you both.

DREW, my little Drewbie! Biggest eyes in the world, widest smile in the universe, dearest laugh from the simplest tickle. All your 100s and 102s in school embarrass me because I was never so

smart, and you're just in first grade! You are the son who would be president, and the best friend of any kid on the block. Your love and natural generosity fills us all and everyone around us. I am proud to be your daddy.

LORI KLIESMET, the love of my life. I think of you every moment I am not with you and can't keep my eyes and hands off of you when I am. God only knows what might have become of me had we not met. I couldn't handle any of this without your unselfish constancy. I pray to God that I return to you the same love you've so unabashedly given to me.

I GOT BY WITH A LITTLE A LOT OF HELP FROM MY FRIENDS

Thanks, MARY GOODBODY for helping me write another one. Why is it that, the busier and more disorganized I get, the more patient you get? You're a great friend and highly valued colleague.

JANE DYSTEL, my agent, is determined to keep me busy, and busy I remain. Many, many thanks for always having us in the right place at the right time. You're truly the very best!

BILL LEBLOND and the team at CHRONICLE BOOKS have become family in a world that was unfamiliar to me. All the poking, prodding, tugging, and nudging result in beautiful, meaningful books. Your sense of design and integrity show on every page. Thanks, Bill. Thanks, AMY TREADWELL. Thanks, MICHAEL WEISBERG. Thanks, everyone. Without you guys it would all just be a bunch of words and misfit recipes.

Thanks to DEBORAH CALLAN, who painstakingly tested every recipe and helped translate them for the home cook. I hope you still like me! I have run you ragged, indeed. Your good sense and good humor are the best!

To SUSIE CUSHNER and her team who photographed the garden and the food. I love how you, JEE, and the ladies are right in tune with all of the truths we love. Destiny intended for you to shoot this book. Thanks for bringing it all to life.

BILL NIMAN has worked damned hard to bring us responsibly raised beef and pork while working to provide the animals a better life in the process. It's refreshing to see someone achieve success while taking us back to a time when there was a realization that a life had to be taken in order to forward our own. One life is no less or more noble than the rest. Thanks for saying so.

The work and words of DIANE and MARLENE HALVERSON have brought to light the truth that all living beings deserve to be treated with dignity. Our own ancestors, whether from Europe, the Middle East, Asia, the Americas, or Africa, mourned the death of the animals they killed by celebrating their lives. From the Germanic hunters of old who arranged twigs in symbolic patterns of respect on the body of the taken animal to the shaman of the Amazon who apologetically considered the life of a fish before it's prepared, our forbears teach us that humans are not the only lives on earth. Thanks, Diane and Marlene, for helping us think better of it.

PAUL WILLIS is a true visionary, a respected intellectual, and a man of dignity and respect. Paul is the hog farmer who taught Bill Niman everything he wanted to know about raising pigs and likely quite a bit more. He's taught me a lot in the short time I've know him, too: how to restore a prairie in your own backyard, and that his mom makes the best damned hog patties any chef could ever hope to eat! The older generation of farmers at the diner in Thornton, Iowa, think he's nuts. We love him that way.

DR. ORAN HESTERMAN and GAIL IMMIG, both through personal action and through their work with the W. K. KELLOGG FOOD AND SOCIETY INITIATIVE, have brought together more good minds and souls in an effort to create a magnificent food future than almost anyone I know. Thanks for teaching us creative tension and what vested community friendships look like. Thanks for the vision.

The first season in my garden, the time spent there with Lori and my children, the great food we cooked from it, and this book itself would not have been possible without the help of some very dedicated, high-quality friends and neighbors. BRUNO and MARTHA GALLACE helped greatly in a number of ways. From Bruno's sage advice, eagle eye (leveling fence posts), and backhoe skills, to Martha taking countless pictures of the garden construction and helping Lori with Drew's broken arm, the Gallace family holds a special place in the heart of the Nischan family.

DAVE O´CONNELL and BOB CONNELLY have always been there. For helping keep an eye on our errant teens and holding up fence posts in the pouring rain, these two gentlemen shall always have a place at the table. It should be noted that Bob grows some damned tasty strawberries and blueberries (about 200 vines and 120 bushes respectively) and Dave has just about every tool an aspiring first-time gardener could need.

FLORENCE FENSKY is the kind, wise, and gentle soul next door. The daughter of the original family who farmed the land where my home and garden now stand, Florence is from a line that can be traced back to Fairfield's Colonial days. She is our cherished neighborhood historian, chock-full of wonderful stories from a better time. She and her siblings were gifted the remaining farmland by their parents who retired from farming in the 1940s. The Fensky children built their homes here and one is now mine. Florence also has an amazing collection of gardening books that she shared with me when I was planning the garden. Thanks, Florence, and please, thank your parents for me.

DREW NIEPORENT is the greatest restaurateur in the world! Drew had the foresight and courage to create Heartbeat, the original restaurant home for my cuisine of well-being. Someone of Drew's accomplishments and stature rarely needs acknowledgment, but he certainly deserves it. I hosed Drew by failing to acknowledge his role in my success when I accepted a James Beard Award in 2004 for *Taste: Pure and Simple*. I was nervous and forgot, and Drew, ever gracious, understood. Nevertheless, so much of my success can be traced to the time I spent working with Drew, MICHAEL BONADIES, MARTY SHAPIRO, and Drew's brother, the one and only TRACEY NIEPORENT. I remain forever grateful to all of them.

PETER STEPHENS and CHRIS LENNON of Elegant Effects in Fairfield, Connecticut, have been steady providers of friendship and inspiration since we moved here in 1989. Peter is an amazing horticulturalist and Chris an excellent chef. It is Peter's garden artistry that started Lori on creating truly meaningful living spaces in every corner of every yard. The four of us have spent many an evening together while Chris and I cooked and Peter and Lori kept pace with wine. During these wonderful times, we've also accomplished a lot: We named Miche Mache, my first restaurant; we formulated the interior design for the restaurant on a shoestring budget; we planned fantastic joint parties; we planned our spring garden; and Lori and I learned to think big and never look back when it comes to building a garden you can live in. Thanks, guys. We love you longtime.

DAVE and AINSLEY JACKSON are farmers who live to make the dream of a better world a reality for everyone. They own and operate Enterprise Farm, a completely organic farm in South Deerfield, Massachusetts. Dave and I were part of the team that started the New American Farmer Initiative along with Gus Schumacher and Michael Batterberry. When we all dreamed of a pure farm-to-restaurant food system, Dave and Ains were the only folks crazy enough and committed enough to drive a truck filled with organic produce from Massachusetts to Manhattan. They also saved our heinies this year by providing us with the good-quality organic seedlings we couldn't grow ourselves for lack of space and a sufficiently sized cold frame. Thanks, dear friends and great advisors. Much love to baby ASA.

GUS SCHUMACHER and MICHAEL BATTERBERRY have to be mentioned in the same breath of gratitude, as my life is so often intertwined with them simultaneously. These two intellectual and spiritual giants are simply a farmer and a writer, yet their significance to a brighter, warmer, and more complete food humanity proves how simple thoughts and deeds lead to greatness. I am grateful that they both speak at once loudly, clearly, and softly with a warm smile. They have so many friends and deserve every one.

DAN BARBER is my chef-hero. His work at Blue Hill in Manhattan and Blue Hill at Stone Barns (Pocantico, NY) is destined to be legendary. Interestingly, Dan walks the walk with every breath, while continually apologizing for not doing enough! Indeed, he has done more in his life (and he's still a youngster) than many of his peers, including yours truly. Dan's truest magic comes in the form of his striking realism. His reality-based, action-oriented approach to solving the problems of a food supply gone mad has molded and formed the surrounding arguments in ways of which even he may be unaware. He is thoughtful, humble, kind, and he also cooks some damned tasty food.

CARL SAFINA is a true warrior for the oceans. His writings in *Song for a Blue Ocean* changed the way I looked at everything that comes from the water. His work with Blue Oceans Institute and a variety of other organizations offers tremendous hope for a future that will include the fish of our childhood. Without Carl and folks like him, a fishless future might truly be right around the corner. You're so damned smart, Carl. And your way is straightforward and very clear. Thanks for reaching so many of us with your great work. Thanks for being such a damned good fisherman.

JOAN GUSSOW is one of the few pioneers for truly growing your own. Her words take us to the heart of our responsibilities to nature and to ourselves. In her book *This Organic Life*, her garden is the main character. Imagine treating a plot of land as a living being. Then again, why should that be hard? It is the truth. Her wisdom, kindness, brilliance, and common sense seem to come directly from the land, even though her land is a humble plot on the banks of the Hudson River in a small suburban outpost of New York City.

Some of my more important thoughts and decisions have lately been shaped by her words. So, Joan, if something blows up on me, it's your fault!

DR. ERIC CHIVIAN can sum up the romance and vibrance of the perfect relationship between mankind and nature through one sip of his cider and a short story about his humble orchard. May the work in his larger orchard, the Center for Health and the Global Environment at Harvard Medical School, rain the fruits of its good work upon us for generations to come. To DR. PAUL EPSTEIN, KAT, and the rest of the gang at the Center, I thank you, my kids thank you, and, in advance, my grandchildren will thank you once they arrive.

LARRY BAIN, a.k.a. Sir Lawrence of Bainia (as well as Larry the Bainiac), is one of the most dedicated minds and spirits in the movement for a brighter food future. His work with NextCourse in San Francisco shows his deep belief that good, wholesome food is a right for all, not a privilege for a few. His humor, genuineness, and warm glow strangely conspire to create a pungency that is, at times, terrible in its effectiveness. Larry makes great points, and each one comes from a pure love of society and the nature that sustains it. Oh, yes. . . society. That would be us. I'd say, "Hats off, dear Larry," but your head would get cold.

ROB SUNDE and LILA GAULT, my dearest friends: Your support and wisdom has been forming my thoughts and actions for years. Rob, rest well. I miss and love you and shall never forget our time spent together. Lila, here's to many more years of high-quality, positive conspiring!

BETH SHEPARD is my "agent of reality" sidekick. There are quite a few things I couldn't do without her dedication and talent. Are we there yet?

All of the folks I worked with during my tenure as a board member of Chefs Collaborative have taught me how to be better and to keep moving forward. The debates were intense and sometimes personal, but the results were fabulous. Thanks and love to you all.

ROZANNE GOLD and MICHAEL WHITEMAN are dear friends and true advisors. Michael, along with Joe Baum, brought us the timeless wonder of Windows on the World, the Rainbow Room, and many more. Rozanne added her special touch to all. She also told me I *must* make my next book about my mother. Here it is. Many, many thanks.

INDEX

TABLE OF EQUIVALENTS

The exact equivalents in the following tables have been rounded for convenience.

LIQUID/DRY MEASURES

U.S.	METRIC
¼ TEASPOON	1.25 MILLILITERS
½ TEASPOON	2.5 MILLILITERS
1 TEASPOON	5 MILLILITERS
1 TABLESPOON (3 TEASPOONS)	15 MILLILITERS
1 FLUID OUNCE (2 TABLESPOONS)	30 MILLILITERS
¼ CUP	60 MILLILITERS
⅓ CUP	80 MILLILITERS
½ CUP	120 MILLILITERS
1 CUP	240 MILLILITERS
1 PINT (2 CUPS)	480 MILLILITERS
1 QUART (4 CUPS, 32 OUNCES)	960 MILLILITERS
1 GALLON (4 QUARTS)	3.84 LITERS
1 OUNCE (BY WEIGHT)	28 GRAMS
1 POUND	454 GRAMS
2.2 POUNDS	1 KILOGRAM

OVEN TEMPERATURE

FAHRENHEIT	CELSIUS	GAS
250	120	½
275	140	1
300	150	2
325	160	3
350	180	4
375	190	5
400	200	6
425	220	7
450	230	8
475	240	9
500	260	10

LENGTH

U.S.	METRIC
⅛ INCH	3 MILLIMETERS
¼ INCH	6 MILLIMETERS
½ INCH	12 MILLIMETERS
1 INCH	2.5 CENTIMETERS